THE
VEGETARIAN
MENU COOKBOOK

THE VEGETARIAN MENU COOKBOOK

by Elsa Michaels

Drake Publishers Inc.
New York

Published in 1973 by
Drake Publishers Inc.
381 Park Avenue South
New York, N.Y. 10016

Library of Congress Cataloging in Publication Data

Michaels, Elsa.
    The vegetarian menu cookbook.

    1. Vegetarianism. 2. Menus. I. Title.
TX837.M55   641.5'636   73-5514
ISBN 0-87749-516-5

Printed in Italy

Prepared and produced for the publisher by BMG Productions, Incorporated

Book Design by Elaine Gongora

All photographs by Jay Mueller and Jordan Rehm of Visual Images,
Palo Alto, California

To my husband,
who inspired me to study
and whose enthusiasm encouraged
me to write this book.

INTRODUCTION

You may wonder how this book came to be written. It all began about thirty years ago when I married a man who was a confirmed vegetarian. He was also a budding architect, and I felt that he was going to need a wife with a flair for entertaining. Here was a real challenge for me. I loved to entertain, but elegant vegetarian cooking was completely new to me. Yes, there were books available, but I could not get excited about them. They seemed to be lacking in so many ways. I decided to tackle the problem in my own way. I studied dietetics for several years and acquired a diploma in Scientific Nutrition. With this knowledge I set out to create my own vegetarian kitchen, style, and original menus. Naturally I experimented a great deal, and whenever I felt I had a successful idea, I made notes. Gradually I began to combine my artistic abilities, my desire for being original, and my kitchen experience. Over the years, the result has produced dinners and parties, both in Europe and in the United States, that have become well known among those who have been guests in our home.

I acquired a reputation and received many requests for recipes. At the same time, I spent a number of years in the commercial art field, where I designed and produced unique settings for many important parties. This led me to resolve that instead of simply writing a vegetarian cookbook, which I had been urged to do for so long, I would also utilize my artistic abilities; thus *The Vegetarian Menu Cookbook* was born.

I have found over the years that many people can produce a vegetarian dish, but there are few who have the knowledge or experience to plan a meal that is nutritionally well balanced as well as being attractive and palatable. For this reason I have concentrated on complete menus rather than on individual dishes. I have chosen thirty-one menus, so when your friends ask you how you can produce variety with such limitations in food selection, you can offer to feed them for a month without repeating a single dish. I have also included a number of vegetarian hors d'oeuvres, necessary to begin any elegant party, and some vegetarian sandwiches to please family and friends.

To help you achieve your own reputation, for party decorating as well as for creativity in the kitchen, I have included, in addition to menus suitable for entertaining at any level of sophistication, twelve original edible centerpieces. These are attractive decorations to complement your table, and your guests will find them conversation pieces.

The menus that I have given you can easily be adapted to everyday meals and need not be limited to party use. You may be a meat-eating family but decide to devote one day a week to vegetarian food. Most of our family eating patterns become monotonous after a while and such a change once a week is welcome.

As you cook through this book, I hope that you will have the satisfaction of being original and different that I have always enjoyed. All menus are kitchen tested many times. All menus are my original combinations; I hope you will move from them to your own. Good luck!

E. H. M.

FOREWORD

LEONARD MICHAELS,
AIA

To most people vegetarianism is a fad that has no place in the established living habits of western man. They cannot imagine what a vegetarian can possibly find to live on and, if asked to prepare a meal for a vegetarian, they will usually produce a collection of several vegetables on a platter, some of which have come straight out of a can. The experienced vegetarian, accustomed to being a member of a minority group, will give a smile of appreciation but will secretly heave a sigh of exasperation. I sometimes wonder whether a few such experiences started my wife on the road to development of the culinary art of vegetarian cooking.

It took a while for her to realize that, in marrying a vegetarian, she had taken a bear by the tail. The philosophical vegetarian is usually also a food reformist, and I was no exception. When she had tired of cooking separate meals for each of us she decided to enter wholeheartedly into the vegetarian fold and to equip herself with a firm foundation of nutritional knowledge on which she could develop her culinary skills. She soon absorbed what was to be learned from available vegetarian recipes, but this did not satisfy her desire to be able to entertain with elegant food. From this point onward she was creating and innovating menus of well-balanced, exciting vegetarian food for our nonvegetarian guests. They responded with amazement and enthusiasm, and came back for seconds and for recipes. Almost without exception they were nonvegetarians, and they were astonished that such gourmet delights could be created without the use of conventional flesh foods.

Over a period of many years I have been presented with all kinds of arguments intended to prove that man is carnivorous by nature and has been equipped for such a diet. Whatever their school of thought, there are many people who, for one reason or another, find it beneficial to vary their diet by having a vegetarian meal, either occasionally or on a regular basis. I remember a very fine vegetarian restaurant in London that catered primarily to such people; after nearly forty years in business it is still doing a roaring trade.

I believe that the menus in this book will give great encouragement to those who like, either occasionally or regularly, to eat vegetarian food, but who have found themselves very limited in their choice of dishes. For those who discover these menus for the first time, vegetarian food may well become an addiction. For those who are always looking for new ways to surprise their guests, I can think of no better way than to try the vegetarian fare with a flair whose magic lives in the pages of this book.

L. M.

GENERAL INFORMATION

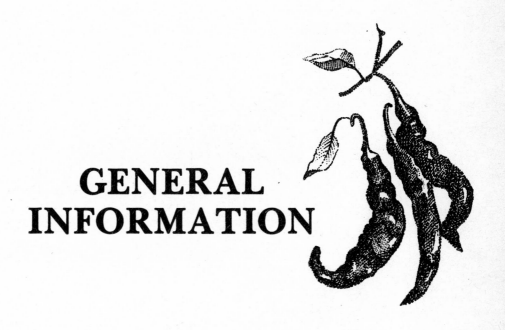

All nuts used in the recipes are unsalted raw nuts unless otherwise stated, and are available at health food stores.

Savita is a trade name for a yeast product to which flavoring has been added. It not only has good food value but is a useful flavoring for soups, sauces, and stews.

Washington Broth is bought in packages of several little envelopes, available at most food stores. It is made in chicken flavor or beef flavor but does not contain any animal product. This seasoning adds flavor to many dishes, and you will find reference to it in many of my recipes.

A good, sturdy, four-sided *grater*, if you do not have a grater attachment for your electric mixer, is an essential kitchen tool.

For your centerpieces you will need some basic items that come in handy for most of the pieces. At any art and floral supply center you will find sheets or shapes of styrofoam, green floral tape, green foil, floral clay, and ribbons. You will also need a very sharp knife for cutting foam, ordinary U-shaped hairpins, and round toothpicks made of wood.

It is also a good idea to collect medium-sized interesting containers in order to have them ready and available when you need them.

When I have not incorporated a candle into a centerpiece, remember that it always looks festive to have candlesticks on each side of a centerpiece.

The menus on the following pages are planned for four people. You will be able to make your own adjustments for more or fewer guests.

HERB GUIDE

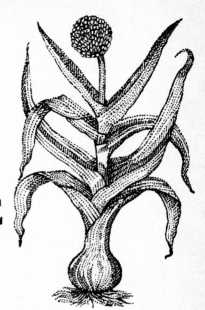

Once you depart from the strong flavors of flesh cooking, you realize the importance of becoming a good cook. If you find this challenge too difficult or there are too many other interests in your life, this book will help you tremendously in taking the burden off your shoulders. Herbs are important to good cooking but essential to vegetarian cooking.

Most herbs have several varieties, both wild and cultivated species. However, I will only mention the most commonly used herbs, and I will not burden you with unnecessary information. My whole book has been selective in its material in order to simplify your task of planning and deciding what and how to prepare a tasty vegetarian meal. Many herbs are beneficial to our well-being as well as adding interest to the meals. If you are unable to grow them in your garden or in flower pots, they are all available in dried form at your food stores.

I must, however, emphasize that regardless of what you are cooking, the addition of herbs should enhance and not dominate your food.

So be gentle until you become familiar with the flavors.

FENNEL

This herb is a native of India, Argentina, and France, and is cultivated in the United States. The United States imports about 300,000 pounds of fennel seed every year. The yellowish-brown seeds are used for flavoring sweet pickles and sauces and the leaves make a pretty garnish for food dishes. The oil taken from the plant is used ·in toilet soaps and perfumes.

MINT

This plant grows in all parts of the world and is known to most of us. It can be grown very easily in your garden or in a flower pot or you can purchase the dried flakes at your food store. Mint has a cool pepperminty flavor and is most commonly used in jellies, fruit juices, candies, peas, and sauces. The leaf, when fresh, is very pretty and the sprigs are often used to decorate fruits, drinks, and desserts. It has a refreshing odor.

PARSLEY

This plant is known to all of us, and those who do not know how to take advantage of using parsley in foods have surely utilized it in decorating their serving platters. All too often the decoration is removed from the food and the parsley thrown away. We should remember that parsley is an excellent source of vitamins A and C as well as being rich in minerals, especially iron. Therefore be generous with this herb, for its flavor enhances most dishes. It is easy to grow and is also available as dried flakes or in ground form.

MARJORAM

Several kinds of marjoram are cultivated in North America; the wild variety is known as oregano. The sweet marjoram has a milder taste than oregano. The leaves, stems, and flowers are available in ground or whole form and add a pleasant flavor to many foods, especially vegetable soups, eggs, and cheese dishes.

BASIL

The most commonly used plant is the sweet basil, which is an annual herb. The leaves flavor soups, salads, and eggs. It is used a great deal in Italian cooking. The flavor is rather sweet and spicy. The herb is available in whole or ground form.

BAY LEAF

This aromatic dried leaf comes from the bay-laurel tree and is sold as a whole leaf. It is a native of the Atlantic coastal areas. The early Greeks used sprigs of bay or laurel to crown the winners of Olympic games. By adding the whole leaf to stews, soups, and sauces, the flavor is greatly enhanced. It is especially good in tomato sauce or juice. Always remove leaf from foods before serving.

CHERVIL

This is a European herb of the parsley family and is used a great deal in French cooking. We use the roots and seeds of this plant for flavoring. It can be purchased in whole or ground form and is most commonly used with cream soups, eggs, and cheese dishes as well as in salads. It is somewhat sweet and mild in flavor.

DILL

This is a hardy plant related to parsley, anise, and caraway. It grows in southeastern Europe, India, and the United States. Dill makes a wonderful addition to salads, cottage cheese, and sauces, especially mayonnaise dressings. The oil from the plant is also used in perfumes. We mostly use the chopped leaves, although the seeds are used for pickling.

OREGANO (WILD MARJORAM)

This herb has a different flavor from that of sweet marjoram and is a member of the mint family with a rather strong, slightly bitter taste. It is good with vegetable stews, nut roasts, and often used in pizzas.

ROSEMARY

You probably know rosemary as an evergreen shrub—so pretty with its purple little flowers that it is often used in landscaping. A member of the mint family, it is a native of the Mediterranean region. The oil from the plant is used in perfumes. To the cook it is available in whole or ground form. It has an aromatic odor and a slightly piny taste. Rosemary is often used in stuffings and nut roasts, and also adds a tasty note to potatoes and cauliflower.

SAGE

This herb belongs to the mint family and originated in the southern part of Europe. Today it is grown throughout North America. In cooking we use the leaves and stems. Sage is most commonly used in stuffings or nut roasts.

SAVORY

Savory should be used sparingly since it has a rather strong, pungent flavor. It is most commonly used with stews, soups, sauces, and eggs.

TARRAGON

The seeds of the tarragon plant are used to flavor pickles, vinegar, and cookies, and is also used in some cooking oils.

THYME

Thyme is a fragrant garden herb; the most commonly used variety is the lemon thyme. It has a delicious flavor and enhances many vegetable dishes, nut roasts, and sauces.

THE
VEGETARIAN
MENU COOKBOOK

EDIBLE
CENTERPIECES

I have mentioned in the General Information section that you will find it useful to acquire a few essentials before starting to prepare your centerpieces. I suggest that you cover all styrofoam with green foil so that when your guests have nibbled at the food in the centerpiece the foam is not visible.

PINEAPPLE FANTASY

Cut one slice off the bottom of the pineapple so that it stands flat, and set it on a small plate. Make small cream-cheese balls with your hands and roll them in the ground almonds. Put them on toothpicks and stick into pineapple here and there. Take some ribbon—the color of your choice—and make untied bows by taking hairpins and securing in center of two or three layers of 3-inch lengths of ribbon. Surround pineapple with fresh, washed leaves.

1 fresh pineapple
1 plate
1 8-ounce package cream cheese
½ cup finely ground almonds
toothpicks
ribbon and hairpins
fresh leaves

FRUIT MEDLEY

Secure styrofoam disk onto base with 4 or 5 toothpicks. Spray foam stand, disk, and fruit with gold paint, but wrap green leaves of pineapple with aluminum foil, newspaper, or some other protection so they do not catch the paint. Allow the paint to dry. Arrange fruit on disk. Pin leaves around disk so foam does not show, and fill in with ribbon bows. Remove protection from pineapple leaves.

1 styrofoam stem base
1 styrofoam disk, 1 inch thick and
     10 inches in diameter
1 pineapple
3 bananas
2 lemons
toothpicks
gold spray paint
leaves
hairpins, plain pins, and ribbon

GRAPE FANTASY

1 styrofoam disk, 2 inches thick, 10
   inches in diameter
green foil, enough to wrap foam
leaves
1 tree branch with firm stem, about
   12 inches high
a few small bunches of grapes
3/4 cup granulated sugar
ribbon and very fine string or cotton
   thread

Wrap styrofoam disk with foil and spread clean leaves over and around it. Remove leaves from branch and press into center of disk. Wash small grape bunches and dip into granulated sugar. Allow to dry and tie to branch with thread wherever you can find a suitable place. Cover up thread or string with ribbon bows.

HERB DELIGHT

Cut a thin layer off top of French bread and hollow out the inside. Line with a foil-covered strip of dampened oasis. Press washed, dried garden herbs into oasis, using scissors to make small holes first because the stems of the herbs are not stiff enough. Use high herbs at one end, finishing up with low parsley at the other end. Insert scissors at an angle into low end of loaf so that your company can snip off herbs if they wish.

1 long loaf of French bread
green foil
1 long oasis strip, to fit inside of loaf
1 small pair of scissors
fresh herbs of your choice (e.g., parsley, dill, mint, chives)

FRAGRANT FLOWERPOT

1 flowerpot
spray paint, if desired
floral clay
styrofoam
toothpicks
9 lemons
3 limes
miniature marshmallows
12 long wood skewers
green floral tape
5 cinnamon sticks
ribbon and hairpins

Take clean flowerpot and if desired spray paint it green or any other color of your choice. Place some floral clay in bottom. Cut a few pieces of styrofoam to fit and place several layers in flowerpot, securing each to the other with toothpicks, until pot is three-quarters filled. Wrap wood skewers with floral tape and secure them at angles in flowerpot. Make lemon and lime "roses." Start by cutting thin slice from stem end of fruit to form base of flower; starting 1/4 inch above base, cut peel around fruit continuously, without removing knife, to form spiral piece of peel. Curl spiral onto base to form flower. Stick onto wrapped skewer, using a miniature marshmallow at top and bottom of flower. This will help to hold it in place and look pretty at the same time. Put a cinnamon stick between flowers here and there. Fill in remaining spaces with hairpin-ribbon bows; no styrofoam must show. If necessary, cover foam with green foil before placing skewers. Spread clean garden leaves around pot.

SUGAR BOWL SURPRISE

1 large sugar bowl with lid
styrofoam disk to fit bowl approximately
floral clay
12 large radishes
12 zucchini sticks
3 carrot sticks
long wood skewers
floral tape
leaves

Place some floral clay at bottom of sugar bowl. Secure the styrofoam disk to clay. Wrap skewers with floral tape. Make radish "roses" by removing root ends from radishes and making cuts around radishes. Chill in ice water with remaining vegetable sticks; this will open up the gashes in the radishes. Leave in ice water for about two hours. Fasten radishes and vegetable sticks to skewers and insert skewers into foam in sugar bowl at different angles. Fill spaces with hairpin-ribbon bows. No foam must show; if necessary cover foam with green foil before securing skewers. Surround bowl with clean leaves and place sugar bowl lid close to bowl at a slant.

TOMATOES IN A TEAPOT

Your teapot should be filled to ¾ full with styrofoam; fasten the styrofoam pieces to one another with toothpicks. Cover with green foil and secure in the pot with floral clay. Wrap the 24 skewers with green floral tape. Make tomato flowers by cutting 5 lines through skin of tomato, about ½-inch downward from stem end. Carefully peel back skin almost to cuts but not quite, so that it does not come off; these form the curled-back petals of the flower. Take off stems and replace with small sprig of fresh parsley. Thread skewer right through tomato and parsley so that parsley is held onto tomato. Use remaining skewers for cheese cubes. Place in foam at angles inside teapot. Fill spaces with hairpin-ribbon bows, leaving a few long ends of ribbon to hang over side of teapot. Surround pot with clean leaves and place lid close to teapot at a slant.

pretty teapot and lid
styrofoam, to fit in teapot
green foil
floral clay
12 firm cherry tomatoes
12 bite-sized cheese cubes
a few fresh sprigs of parsley
24 long wood skewers
floral tape
ribbon, hairpins, toothpicks

WINTER SCOOP

Spray leaves gold and allow to dry. Wrap foam boat in green foil. Stand up against candle in holder at an angle, hollow side up. You will have to find a way of securing top end of boat to candle holder, depending on what kind of holder you have. Remember you can thread anything through foam and tie to holder. If it shows, cover up with ribbon. Should you be unable to get hold of a foam boat, you can use a disk instead. Make an arrangement of Indian corn and gourds from top of boat down to table, securing pieces with toothpicks onto foam. Place a piece of dried fruit at end of each long wood skewer and fasten here and there into foam between gourds and corn.. Make some hairpin-ribbon bows and attach them where you feel they are most needed. The whole appearance of this centerpiece should lead down from top of candle to table at an angle. Surround with gold leaves.

1 fat candle and tall holder,
    together about 12 inches high
1 styrofoam boat, long enough to
    reach halfway down from can-
    dle to table
green foil
long wood skewers
green floral tape
gourds
Indian corn
assorted dried fruits
gold spray paint
ribbon, hairpins, toothpicks

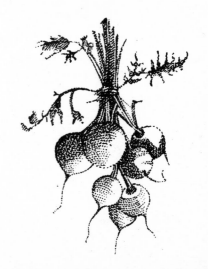

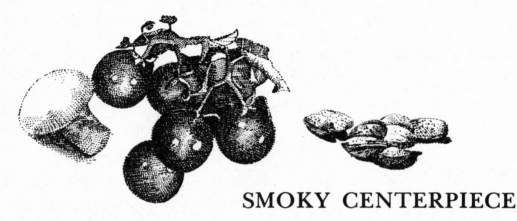

SMOKY CENTERPIECE

1 pretty ice bucket, not too high
small piece of dry ice, kept in
    freezer until ½ hour before
    dinner. Can be bought in ice
    cream stores.
1 styrofoam disk, a little smaller
    than inside of ice bucket
1 package long wooden skewers
floral tape, green
1 jar almond-stuffed green olives
8 cheese cubes
9 cherry tomatoes
ribbon, hairpins, toothpicks

Prepare your centerpiece on the styrofoam disk. Because the dry ice has to be placed at the bottom of ice bucket one-half hour before dinner, the centerpiece will be inserted just before dinner is served. Wrap wood skewers with green floral tape and secure at angles in foam disk. Attach a cheese cube or olive or tomato to each skewer and fasten the skewers to the styrofoam, mixing the colors. If the ice bucket is too deep for the skewers to show, make a few layers of foam disks, securing each to the other with toothpicks. Cut a few ribbon lengths 12 inches long, secure to foam at center point with hairpin, and let hang over side of bucket. When you have placed dry ice underneath the foam disks, steam will rise all around the centerpiece. Your guests will be fascinated.

APPLE TEMPTATION

Wrap styrofoam disk and cone with green foil and secure cone on center of disk with four toothpicks. Cut a 1½-inch piece off top of cone with a very sharp knife and place candleholder on resulting flat surface. Pull stems off apples and replace with two toothpicks to each apple. Fasten apples around cone in circles, about 3 rows. Fill in all spaces with ribbon-and-hairpin bows secured into foam until no foam is visible. Surround plate with fresh clean garden leaves.

1 styrofoam disk, 2 inches thick and 10 inches in diameter
1 styrofoam cone, 6 inches high
green foil, enough for wrapping the styrofoam
toothpicks
1 small candleholder with three prongs to stick into top of styrofoam cone
1 candle to fit into holder
10 to 12 apples, red, polished
ribbon and hairpins
leaves

NUT BASKET

1 medium-sized basket with handle
leaves
gold spray paint
ribbon
all kinds of nuts in their shells
1 pair of nutcrackers

Spray basket and garden leaves with gold paint and allow to dry. Place gold leaves around basket and fill basket with nuts. Rest nutcrackers at an angle to basket. Tie a long piece of ribbon to each side of handle and let it flow over leaves onto table.

SEASHELL

1 pineapple
1 package of wood skewers
1 seashell, the size of a large
    ashtray
styrofoam, a piece small enough to
    fit inside seashell
green foil, enough to wrap foam
floral clay
ribbon and hairpins
leaves

Remove pineapple shell and prepare bite-sized pieces. Secure a wooden skewer to each piece. Cover styrofoam with green foil and place in seashell (exact fit not necessary). Use a small piece of floral clay to secure foam in shell. Stick pineapple pieces into foam at angles. Fill in spaces with hairpin-ribbon bows and surround shell with clean garden leaves.

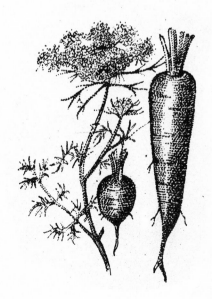

HORS D'OEUVRES

CHEESE STRAWS

4 ounces butter
1 cup flour
1 cup grated sharp cheddar cheese
2 eggs plus 1 yolk
1/2 cup poppy seeds
onion salt and pepper to taste

Grate butter into flour, add grated cheese, salt, and pepper. Work in 2 eggs with knife until well mixed and press dough flat onto baking sheet. Flour your hands generously and this will make the even distribution of the dough simpler. Pastry should be about 1/4 inch thick on baking sheet. Brush with beaten egg yolk and sprinkle with poppy seed. Bake in moderate oven (350°) for about 30 minutes or until light brown. When cool cut into 2 inch long strips or longer if you prefer. Serve with avocado dip.

STUFFED CHERRY TOMATOES

24 firm cherry tomatoes
5 egg yolks
1 tablespoon mayonnaise
1/4 teaspoon mustard
1/4 cup chopped chives
onion salt and pepper to taste

Cut thin slice off top of tomatoes. Remove seeds. Mash yolks of egg with mayonnaise, chives, mustard, onion salt, and pepper, and fill tomatoes generously. Replace tops of tomatoes.

AVOCADO DIP

Peel and remove stones from avocados. Mash avocados with rest of ingredients and cover tightly until served. Serve with cheese straws.

4 ripe avocados
2 tablespoons lemon juice
⅓ cup chopped green onions
1 tablespoon mayonnaise
onion salt, pepper, sugar to taste

STUFFED CELERY PIECES

Boil eggs until hard and remove yolks. Mash up yolks with mayonnaise, mustard, onion salt, dill weed. Stuff celery pieces with mixture. Sprinkle with riced egg whites and paprika.

24 2-inch-long pieces celery
6 eggs
2 tablespoons mayonnaise
1 teaspoon prepared mustard
1 tablespoon dill weed
onion salt
paprika

GARLIC CHEESE BALLS

1 small package Velveeta cheese
1 4-ounce package cream cheese
¼ teaspoon garlic salt
¼ cup finely chopped pecans
onion salt, paprika
cocktail sticks

Thoroughly mix and mash up all ingredients except paprika and nuts. Add chopped nuts and shape into small cocktail-sized balls. Roll in paprika and refrigerate until ready to use and then place on cocktail sticks.

CREAM CHEESE-PINEAPPLE DIP

1 8-ounce package cream cheese
2 tablespoons well-drained crushed
    pineapple
1 teaspoon finely chopped mint
onion salt

Blend all the ingredients and serve with crackers.

MUSHROOM PUFFS

Make puffs by melting 4 ounces margarine in 1 cup water. Over heat, add, quickly one cup flour, stirring vigorously until you have a smooth, thick paste that leaves sides of saucepan. Add eggs, one at a time and mix thoroughly. Add a little onion salt and pepper. Grease cookie sheet and drop heaped teaspoons of dough on sheet. Bake at 420° for 15 minutes and another 15 minutes at 325°. Allow to cool.

Make mushroom filling by melting 2 ounces margarine in a pan. Add 2 tablespoons of flour, stirring all the time. Add ½ cup water and the wine. Boil, stirring all the time, until mixture thickens. Chop up mushroom caps and fry in 1 ounce margarine with chopped parsley, a little onion salt, and pepper. Add to filling. Slice tops off puffs and fill puffs with mushroom mixture. Replace tops and serve warm.

7 ounces margarine
1½ cups water
1 cup plus 2 tablespoons flour for filling
3 eggs
1 tablespoon wine
12 mushroom caps
2 teaspoons parsley, chopped
onion salt and pepper to taste

PIQUANT STUFFED MUSHROOMS

24 large mushroom caps
1 package chicken-flavored Wash-
*   ington Broth*
1 teaspoon celery salt
2 teaspoons ground walnuts
1 teaspoon Worcestershire sauce
1 teaspoon chopped parsley
½ teaspoon lemon juice
1 teaspoon chopped capers
½ cup fine bread crumbs
2 ounces butter

Remove stems from mushrooms and cook both in water with Washington Broth for about 15 minutes. Drain well and reserve caps. Chop stems very fine, mix with celery salt, ground walnuts, Worcestershire sauce, parsley, lemon juice, and capers. Warm this filling in 1 ounce butter. Fill caps, sprinkle with bread crumbs and dot with remaining butter. Broil until light brown. Serve warm.

ONION PUFFS

24 slices bread
½ cup mayonnaise
½ cup chopped green onions
½ cup Parmesan cheese

Cut out bread rounds with a small glass used upside down and toast rounds on cookie sheet until lightly browned. Mix mayonnaise with green onions and put a heaping teaspoon on each toast round. Sprinkle generously with Parmesan cheese and broil. Serve hot.

MUSHROOM ROSES

24 slices bread
14 large mushroom caps
¼ cup chopped chives
1 ounce butter
1 8-ounce package cream cheese
onion salt and pepper to taste

Cut out toast rounds with a small glass used upside down. Toast rounds on cookie sheet until lightly browned. Chop mushrooms very finely and cook in butter with chives, onion salt, and pepper. Place a generous teaspoon of this mixture on each toast round. Mash up softened cream cheese. Add 3 cream cheese petals to edge of each toast round over mushrooms, using pointed end of teaspoon to form petals. Broil until petals are lightly browned and serve hot.

HOT OLIVE PASTRIES

Blend cheese with softened butter. Using fingers, mix with flour until well blended. Add onion salt and pepper. Grease your hands a little with oil and work dough around thoroughly *dry* olives. This is not an easy operation, but patience will reward you. Place on greased cookie sheet and bake for 15 minutes in 400° oven. Serve warm on cocktail sticks. This can be prepared ahead of time except for baking.

1 cup grated Parmesan cheese
2 ounces butter
1/2 cup flour
24 olives with almond stuffing
onion salt and pepper to taste

HOT PICKLE BROIL

Cut out bread rounds with a small glass used upside down. Toast rounds on cookie sheet in oven until lightly browned. Place a well-drained pickle slice on each toast round. Baste lightly with oil and sprinkle generously with Parmesan cheese. Broil and serve hot.

24 slices bread
24 slices sweet pickle
1/2 cup grated Parmesan cheese
1/2 cup oil

CUCUMBER ROLL-UPS

Cut thin slices of unpeeled cucumber into a bowl. Sprinkle with onion salt and dill and allow to stand for an hour. This will make slices softer and more pliable. Then roll one slice of cucumber around a cheese cube and put on cocktail sticks so that stick secures the two ends of cucumber.

1 small cucumber, the less seeds
    the better
1 teaspoon dill weed
24 small cubes of your favorite
    cheese
onion salt
cocktail sticks

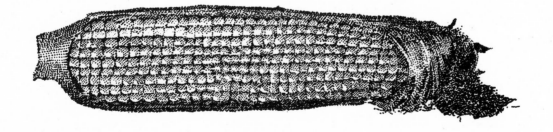

15 VEGETARIAN GOURMET SANDWICHES

Many of us with families for whom we provide sandwiches welcome new ideas for sandwich spreads to break the monotony. We must be conscious of the fact that these meals should be tasty as well as healthy. Relax and let me guide you through fifteen easy-to-prepare sandwich fillings featuring combinations of proteins and vegetables with herb flavors you and your family or guests will enjoy.

VEGETABLE SANDWICH

Grate raw cauliflower and blend with just enough mayonnaise to make spread. Add a little dill weed, salt, and pepper, and spread over bread. Cover with some endive. This filling is especially tasty with thin-sliced black bread.

EGG-TOMATO MIX

Take a few hard-boiled egg yolks (you can use the remaining hard-boiled whites of the eggs for a salad) and mash with just enough mayonnaise to make a spread. Add 1/4 teaspoon of prepared mustard and a small quantity of peeled, chopped tomatoes, a little chopped chives, salt and pepper to taste. Make sure mixture is not too thin; the amount of mayonnaise you use will control this.

VITAMIN A SANDWICH

Grate some peeled, raw carrots. Mix with enough cream cheese to blend into a spread. Add a dash of ginger and some raisins. A leaf of butter lettuce will complete this sandwich.

SWISS CHEESE SANDWICH PLUS IRON

Grate some Swiss cheese and add enough ketchup to blend into a spread. Finely chop generous quantity of raw spinach leaves and add to cheese spread. This sandwich is especially good on rye bread.

NUT SANDWICH

Purchase a jar of cashew-nut butter at your local health food store. Place some nut butter in a small bowl. Add diced raw cucumber (seeds removed) and a little dill weed. Serve with romaine lettuce over spread.

TASTY CHEESE AND ENERGY SANDWICH

Wash and dry small quantity of watercress. Grate cheddar cheese and mix with just enough ketchup to blend into a spread. Add coarsely chopped watercress and a dash of marjoram.

EGG AND ZUCCHINI SANDWICH

Grate some small raw zucchinis, leaving on the skin, and set aside. Mash hard-boiled eggs with just enough mayonnaise to make a spread, and add grated zucchini, some chopped parsley, and salt and pepper to taste.

TOMATO-SCRAMBLE SANDWICH

Beat two or three raw eggs, depending on how many sandwiches you wish to make. Add a little salt and pepper and scramble in frying pan with a little butter. Allow to cool and spread on bread. Cover with tomato slices and sprinkle with a little basil. This sandwich is very good on toasted bread.

SWEET-TOOTH SANDWICH

Soften cream cheese at room temperature. Add finely chopped dates, a little sugar, and chopped pecan nuts. This sandwich is very good on raisin bread.

PROTEIN SANDWICH

Purchase a jar of almond butter at your local health food store. Mix some of the almond butter with finely chopped green onions. Spread on bread and cover with butter lettuce.

AVOCADO SANDWICH

Mash one ripe avocado with a little fresh lemon juice and a small amount of mayonnaise, making sure mixture is not runny. Add a little sugar, salt, and pepper to taste. Spread on bread and cover with butter lettuce.

SAVITA SANDWICH

Soften some butter or margarine at room temperature. Add 1/2 teaspoon of Savita (see General Information) and blend to a smooth brown butter. Top with generous amount of alfalfa seed sprouts (available in packages at most food stores and health food stores).

CREAM CHEESE -CARAWAY SANDWICH

Soften cream cheese at room temperature. Add some finely chopped celery pieces, salt, pepper, and sprinkle with a little caraway seed. Spread on bread and cover with thin slices of raw cucumber.

CURRY SANDWICH

Mash some hard-boiled eggs with a little mayonnaise. Add a generous dash of curry powder and some chopped chives. Spread on bread and cover with lettuce.

COTTAGE CHEESE SANDWICH

Drain some cole slaw very thoroughly. Mix some creamed cottage cheese with finely chopped green onions and some finely chopped sweet gherkins. Spread on bread and cover with well-drained cole slaw. It may be necessary to wrap cole slaw in cheesecloth in order to squeeze all liquid out of it.

MENU 1

PINEAPPLE BOATS
BAKED STUFFED CABBAGE ROLLS
TOMATO SAUCE
MINTED PEAS
GOURMET POTATOES
APPLE-WINE FRITTERS

Much has been heard and written about the art of cooking, but not enough about the complementary art of "planning a meal."

A meal should be nutritious, it should delight the palate, and it should have visual appeal; it must be conceived as a whole composition that satisfies these conditions without the kind of imbalance that results in an excess of calories or leaves the consumer in a state of stupor by the time he leaves the table.

HELPFUL HINT
If you decide to serve Menu 1 by candlelight, put your candles in the freezer compartment of your refrigerator overnight and place on the dinner table just before serving. The candles will burn more evenly and last longer.

PINEAPPLE BOATS

Cut the fresh pineapple in half lengthwise, cutting right through leaves. Cut each half again into quarters, including leaves. Loosen pineapple with serrated knife and cut into 5 or 6 pieces. Sprinkle each quarter with a little brown sugar.

2 fresh pineapples
2 tablespoons brown sugar

BAKED STUFFED CABBAGE ROLLS

Place ten outer cabbage leaves in a pan and pour boiling water over them to cover. Let them stand for five minutes, remove water. In 1 ounce margarine, fry chopped onions until golden brown. Mix fried onions with ground nuts, cooked rice, grated cheddar cheese, and parsley. Add the eggs, ketchup, onion salt, and pepper, and mix well. Place a heaping tablespoon of this mixture on each cabbage leaf. Fold leaves from four sides and place in a greased, ovenproof casserole dish. Top with fresh tomato sauce (see below), and bake, uncovered, in a moderate oven (350°) for approximately 40 minutes or until light brown on top.

1 green cabbage
1 ounce margarine
1/2 cup chopped onion
1 cup ground cashew nuts
1 cup cooked rice
1/2 cup grated cheddar cheese
1 teaspoon chopped parsley
2 eggs
1 tablespoon ketchup
onion salt and pepper to taste

TOMATO SAUCE

Melt margarine in saucepan and fry chopped onion and tomatoes for 5 minutes. Add flour and stir until smooth. Continue stirring and add 1 cup water and the Dubonnet. Bring to boil until it thickens and let it simmer for a few minutes. Strain sauce and add Washington Broth, onion salt, pepper, oregano, and sugar. Pour over cabbage rolls.

2 ounces margarine
1/2 cup chopped onion
5 medium-sized tomatoes, chopped coarsely
2 tablespoons flour
1 cup water
2 tablespoons Dubonnet
1 package chicken-flavored Washington Broth
1/4 tablespoon oregano
onion salt, pepper, sugar to taste

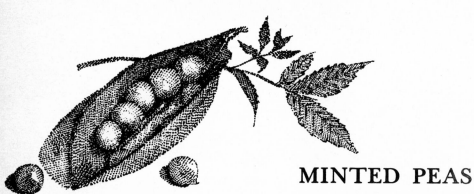

MINTED PEAS

2 pounds fresh peas
1 tablespoon chopped fresh mint
2 ounces margarine
¼ teaspoon nutmeg
onion salt and pepper to taste

Shell peas. Fry chopped mint in hot margarine and boil with 2 cups water. Add peas and cook until tender. Before serving, drain excess liquid and add onion salt, pepper, and nutmeg.

GOURMET POTATOES

6 medium-sized potatoes
2 ounces margarine
1 tablespoon chopped parsley
½ cup milk
2 eggs, beaten
onion salt and pepper to taste

Cook potatoes in skins, peel while still warm, cut into slices, and place in greased ovenproof dish. Melt margarine, mix with milk, eggs, parsley, onion salt, and pepper and pour over potatoes. Sprinkle with a little more onion salt and bake uncovered in moderate oven (350°) for approximately 30 minutes, or until lightly brown on top. This can be baked at the same time as the cabbage rolls.

APPLE-WINE FRITTERS

4 large green apples
2 cups flour
4 eggs, separated
½ cup dry Vermouth
½ cup honey
1 cup oil
½ cup granulated sugar
pinch of salt

Mix flour, Vermouth, egg yolks, honey, and pinch of salt to a smooth consistency. Beat egg whites until stiff and fold into batter. Peel apples, take out center core, and cut into ¼-inch slices. Dip into batter and fry in hot oil until golden brown on both sides. Drain. Serve warm and sprinkle generously with granulated sugar.

MENU 2

WALDORF SALAD
EGGPLANT-CHEESE SURPRISE
GLAZED CARROTS
CURRIED RICE
BAKED STUFFED APPLES

You will have discovered by now the variety of foods and flavors available to the vegetarian cook. It is of no concern whether you are a confirmed vegetarian, whether your doctor has told you to eliminate meat from your diet, or whether you are entertaining vegetarian guests and it would be fun for all to join. If the latter is the case, you will have no regrets, but you may be asked for a repeat performance.

HELPFUL HINT
Create the illusion of the effortless hostess: there is no last-minute preparation involved in this menu. The Waldorf salad will taste even better if prepared the day before. The remaining courses can be prepared well ahead of dinner time and reheated when needed.

WALDORF SALAD

Core, peel, and cut apples into small pieces. Add chopped celery, lemon juice, drained beets, mayonnaise, and pecans. Mix lightly, adding sugar to taste. Cover and refrigerate for at least 2 hours. Before serving, drain excess liquid. Serve in individual salad bowls, inserting a thin slice of lemon in center of each salad.

3 apples
1 small can diced beets
¾ cup chopped pecans
1½ cups chopped celery
3 tablespoons mayonnaise
juice of 1 lemon
sugar to taste

EGGPLANT-CHEESE SURPRISE

Cut eggplant into 8 ¼-inch-thick slices. Place 1 slice of cheese between 2 slices of eggplant, trimming cheese to fit sandwich. Beat egg and milk, adding onion salt and pepper. Dip eggplant sandwich into egg mixture; coat with fine bread crumbs on all sides. Cook on both sides in hot oil until brown and until cheese has melted.

1 medium-sized eggplant
4 slices American cheese
1 egg
¼ cup milk
1 cup bread crumbs
1 cup oil
onion salt and pepper to taste

GLAZED CARROTS

Peel and cut carrots into thin slices. Cook in a little boiling water until tender. Drain. Melt butter; add sugar, ginger, and parsley and pour over drained carrots.

2 pounds carrots
1 ounce butter
1 tablespoon brown sugar
¼ teaspoon ginger
1 tablespoon chopped parsley

CURRIED RICE

1½ cups rice
½ cup chopped onion
2 ounces margarine
1 teaspoon curry powder
½ cup seedless raisins
    (soaked and drained)
1 teaspoon brown sugar
onion salt and pepper to taste

Cook rice in boiling water until tender. Drain. Fry chopped onion in melted margarine. Add curry powder, raisins, onion salt, pepper, and sugar. Cook for about 5 minutes and add to drained rice, mixing well.

BAKED STUFFED APPLES

4 green apples
½ cup pitted, chopped prunes
½ cup chopped pecans
¾ cup brown sugar
¾ cup water
juice of 1 lemon

Wash apples and remove center core. Place in ovenproof dish. Stuff center of each apple with mixture of chopped prunes and pecans. Boil water, add lemon juice and sugar, and pour over apples. Bake uncovered in moderate oven (350° for approximately 45 minutes). Apples should be tender but not falling apart; time of baking may vary according to apples.

MENU 3

ARTICHOKE SALAD
SWISS CHARD FRITTERS
WITH CHEESE SAUCE
STUFFED ACORN SQUASH
CHERRY SPONGE WITH CREAM

The French saying *chacun à son goût* has to be respected. We are all entitled to our likes and dislikes, but Menu 3 is a real tongue-tickler. You will not want to miss it.

HELPFUL HINT

In this age when cigarette smoking is offensive to many, yet some of your guests will smoke, you can eliminate lingering cigarette or cigar odors by waxing your ashtrays. You will also find it much easier to clean them after the guests have left.

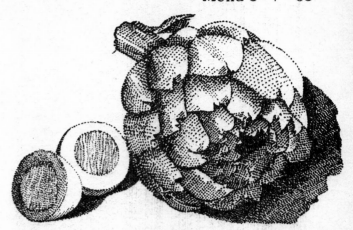

ARTICHOKE SALAD

Boil artichokes until just tender. Drain. Cut off tender parts of leaves and slice bottoms into fine slices. Do not use prickly parts of leaves or soft, bitter part on top of bottom. Shred lettuce onto individual salad plates and place trimmed artichoke pieces in center of each plate. Rice the egg and decorate each salad. Make French dressing by mixing oil, vinegar, dill, onion salt, pepper, and sugar, and pour over each salad.

4 large artichokes
1 head lettuce
1 hard boiled egg
1/2 cup oil
3 tablespoons vinegar
1/2 teaspoon dill weed
onion salt, pepper, and sugar to
    taste

SWISS CHARD FRITTERS

Make fritter batter by mixing eggs, flour, milk, melted margarine, soya flour, onion salt, and pepper. Wash, dry, and chop Swiss chard and add to batter along with chopped onion. Heat oil; drop two tablespoons of batter at a time into hot oil and fry quickly until brown on both sides. Drain on paper towel. Top with cheese sauce (below) and serve with acorn squash (below).

1 cup flour
2/3 cup milk
2 eggs
1 teaspoon soya flour
1 ounce melted margarine
2 cups chopped Swiss chard leaves
1 chopped onion
1/2 cup oil
onion salt and pepper to taste

CHEESE SAUCE

Melt margarine, add flour and milk, and bring to boil, stirring all the time until sauce thickens. Add cheese, onion salt, and pepper. Take off the stove and mix in mustard. Serve over fritters.

2 ounces margarine
2 tablespoons flour
1 1/4 cups milk
1 cup grated cheddar cheese
1 teaspoon mustard
onion salt and pepper to taste

STUFFED ACORN SQUASH

2 small acorn squash
2 ounces butter
1 chopped onion
3 apples, peeled and diced
1/2 teaspoon cinnamon
2 tablespoons brown sugar
1 tablespoon sherry
2 tablespoons almonds, sliced and
    toasted

Cut the acorn squash in halves and remove seeds. Arrange in baking pan, cut side down. Add 1/2 inch of water and bake in 400° oven until tender, about 20 minutes. Cut round side of squash to flat surface and turn squash over to fill with apple mixture.

For apple filling, melt butter and fry chopped onion until golden. Add apples, cinnamon, sugar and sherry, and mix it all. Fill squash with mixture and bake another 15 minutes in 400° oven until apples are tender. Top with toasted sliced almonds before serving with fritters.

CHERRY SPONGE WITH CREAM

3 eggs
3 1/2 tablespoons granulated sugar,
    plus 1 teaspoon for cream
3 1/2 tablespoons flour
1 cup pitted cherries (if canned
    cherries are used, drain well)
1 cup whipping cream
1 teaspoon cherry liqueur

Beat sugar with egg yolks in electric mixer until lemon-colored. In separate bowl beat egg whites stiff and fold in yolk mixture. Fold in flour lightly. Pour into ungreased spring-form cake pan and scatter cherries over top. Bake in moderate oven (350°) for approximately 20 minutes or until sponge is light brown. Serve with cream that has been whipped with 1 teaspoon sugar and the cherry liqueur.

MENU 4

BROILED SHERRIED GRAPEFRUIT
PROTEIN BROIL
MUSHROOM SAUCE
BROILED TOMATO SLICES
SOYA RICE
FRIED FRUIT COMPOTE

This dinner will convince your nonvegetarian friends that there is plenty of protein available in the vegetarian larder.

HELPFUL HINT
You have some grating of cheese and vegetables to cope with in this menu. When it comes to grating, you will find it a lot easier if the foods to be grated are cold, whether your grater is an attachment to your electric mixer or a hand grater.

BROILED SHERRIED GRAPEFRUIT

Prepare grapefruit halves by loosening sections with special grapefruit knife on all sides. Sprinkle with brown sugar and pour over this one teaspoon sherry on each half. Broil briefly until brown specks appear on outer rind. Serve hot.

2 pink grapefruits
2 teaspoons brown sugar
4 teaspoons sweet sherry

PROTEIN BROIL

Reserve bread crumbs. Mix remaining ingredients thoroughly. Add onion salt and pepper and form into small flat hamburgers. Coat with bread crumbs and place on broiling pan that has been greased. Broil approximately 4 minutes each side, until brown. Serve with mushroom sauce.

1 cup finely ground cashew nuts
1 cup grated cheddar cheese
1 cup grated cauliflower
1/4 cup finely chopped parsley
2 teaspoons soya flour
1/2 ounce margarine
1/4 teaspoon Savita
1/2 teaspoon thyme
2 eggs
1 cup bread crumbs
onion salt and pepper to taste

MUSHROOM SAUCE

Fry the sliced mushrooms and chopped onions in the butter until golden brown; put aside. Add flour to melted margarine and mix until smooth. Add 1½ cups cold water and sherry. Heat, stirring all the time, until sauce thickens. Add mushrooms and onions. Add bay leaf, chives, broth, onion salt and pepper. Cook gently for 10 minutes, stirring all the time. Remove bay leaf and serve over protein broil.

1 ounce butter
1 cup fresh sliced mushrooms
1/2 cup chopped onions
2 ounces margarine
2 tablespoons flour
1½ cups water
1 tablespoon sherry
1 bay leaf
1/4 cup chopped chives
1 package chicken-flavored Washington Broth
onion salt and pepper to taste

BROILED TOMATO SLICES

6 firm tomatoes
1/4 cup oil
2 teaspoons vinegar
1/2 cup grated Parmesan cheese
1/2 teaspoon garlic salt

Cut tomatoes in thick slices. Place on broiling pan. Prepare basting mixture by adding vinegar and garlic salt to oil; mix. Baste tomatoes and sprinkle with Parmesan cheese. Broil until lightly brown.

SOYA RICE

1 1/2 cups rice
water
1/2 ounce margarine
3 teaspoons soy sauce
onion salt and pepper to taste

Boil rice in water and margarine. When tender, drain excess water. Add soy sauce, onion salt, and pepper.

FRIED FRUIT COMPOTE

1 banana
2 eating apples
1/2 cup pitted prunes
1/2 cup seedless raisins
2 peaches
juice of 1 lemon
1 ounce margarine
1/2 cup water
1 teaspoon honey
1 1/2 tablespoons brown sugar

Peel and slice fruit and cook in melted margarine for 5 minutes. Add lemon juice, 1/2 cup water, brown sugar, and honey. Cover and steam for another 5 minutes. Serve warm.

MENU 5

ONION SOUP
CHEESE CROQUETTES WITH
RED CURRANT JELLY SAUCE
CUCUMBERS WITH DILL
POTATO SNOW
PEARS WITH CARAMEL SAUCE

This dinner is one of my favorites, and I know you will enjoy it all. I have deliberately kept my soup recipe simple in order to encourage a return to the lost art of soup-making without meat stock. If you follow my instructions your guests will never know that meat bones did not travel through the pot.

HELPFUL HINT

Remember that food cools quickly. Plates and platters should be heated. A piping hot meal is so much more attractive.

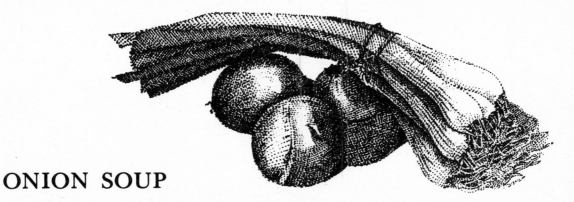

ONION SOUP

Peel and slice vegetables. Fry in melted margarine for 5 minutes. Add 4 cups water and Washington Broth, Savita, onion salt, and pepper. Simmer for 45 minutes. Strain through sieve, pressing as many of the vegetables through strainer as you can, or use blender. Garnish with chopped chives before serving.

2 ounces margarine
4 onions
1 bunch green onions
1 potato
2 packages chicken-flavored Washington Broth
½ teaspoon Savita
¼ teaspoon basil
onion salt and pepper to taste
½ cup chopped chives

CHEESE CROQUETTES

Stir flour into melted margarine. Make a smooth mixture and add milk, stirring all the time while it comes to a boil and thickens, leaving sides of saucepan. Add egg yolk, cheese, marjoram, parsley, onion salt, and pepper and cook for two minutes, stirring vigorously until all is blended. Chill. When cold, shape into croquettes. Dip them into beaten egg and coat with bread crumbs. Heat oil and fry croquettes slowly until golden on all sides and cooked. You will find it helpful to turn croquettes with two forks.

3 ounces margarine
½ cup flour
1 cup milk
1 egg plus 1 egg yolk
1 tablespoon chopped parsley
1 cup grated cheddar cheese
¼ teaspoon marjoram
2 cups bread crumbs
1 egg, beaten
¾ cup oil
onion salt and pepper to taste

RED CURRANT JELLY SAUCE

Mix while heating and serve with croquettes.

¾ cup red currant jelly
2 tablespoons lemon juice

CUCUMBERS WITH DILL

3 cucumbers
2 tablespoons light cream
2 tablespoons chopped green onions
2 teaspoons chopped dill weed
1 ounce butter
onion salt and pepper to taste

Peel and remove seeds of cucumbers and cut into cubes. Fry green onions in butter. Stew with cucumbers in a little boiling water for about ½ hour. Drain excess water. Before serving, add light cream, dill, onion salt, and pepper.

POTATO SNOW

6 medium-sized potatoes
¼ cup milk
1 ounce margarine
onion salt and pepper

Peel potatoes and slice. Boil in a little water until tender. Drain. Add margarine, milk, onion salt, and pepper, and mash very fine over heat.

PEARS IN CARAMEL SAUCE

1½ pounds fresh pears
⅔ cup brown sugar
1 tablespoon lemon juice
1 cup water
½ cup sherry

CARAMEL SAUCE
½ cup brown sugar
½ cup water
½ pint heavy cream, stiffly beaten

Peel and core pears. Add 1 cup water, sherry, lemon juice, and ⅔ cup sugar, and boil about 30 minutes until pears are tender. If there is much liquid left, drain off excess because caramel sauce is fairly thin.

To make caramel sauce, stir ½ cup brown sugar in dry saucepan over low heat until dark brown and moist. Add ½ cup water and boil a few minutes, stirring the sugar and water until all is dissolved. When cool, mix with stiffly beaten whipped cream. Serve with pears.

MENU 6

COLE SLAW AND CHESTNUT SALAD
SPINACH AND MUSHROOM CREPES
IN CHEESE SAUCE
POTATO PATTIES
RICE SOUFFLE PUDDING
WITH FRUIT GLAZE

Hostesses seem to shy away from crepes. Actually, the following recipe is foolproof, and because you can make it ahead of time there is no last minute tension involved. You can freeze the whole dish, complete with cheese sauce poured over the crepes. Just wrap the casserole dish in foil. The only *must* is a very small, crepe-sized frying pan.

HELPFUL HINT

If you have favorite recipes written on odd cards that get handled a great deal while your hands are busy in the kitchen, cover the lines with clear Scotch tape. It will protect the writing from wet fingers that cause smudges.

COLE SLAW AND CHESTNUT SALAD

Shred cabbage and grate carrot. Mix up in bowl and pour boiling water over them. Add chestnuts, vinegar, oil, parsley, and seasoning. Marinate in refrigerator for at least 1 hour. Drain and spoon into individual bowls.

1 small green cabbage
1 carrot
1/2 cup boiling water
1 small can chestnuts
1/2 cup vinegar
1/2 cup salad oil
1/2 cup chopped parsley
onion salt, pepper, and sugar to taste

SPINACH AND MUSHROOM CREPES

Beat eggs with milk, melted butter, and seasonings. Add flour, gradually beating until smooth. Refrigerate for 1/2 hour. Use one tablespoon of batter per crepe and fry quickly on both sides in lightly oiled skillet. Turn out flat onto a piece of waxed paper and prepare filling.

CREPES

2 eggs
1 cup milk
2 tablespoons melted butter
1/2 cup flour
1/2 cup oil for frying
onion salt and pepper to taste

Fry chopped onion and sliced mushrooms in melted margarine for 2 or 3 minutes. Add flour, Washington Broth, spinach, water, and sherry. Boil, stirring all the time, until mixture thickens and is smooth. Cool. Place 1 tablespoon of vegetable mixture in center of each crepe. Fold crepe on 4 sides and place in buttered ovenproof dish.

FILLING

2 ounces margarine
1/2 cup chopped onion
1 cup sliced mushrooms
1 tablespoon flour
1 package chicken-flavored Washington Broth
1/2 cup water
1 1/2 cups spinach, cooked, drained, and chopped
1/2 tablespoon sherry
onion salt and pepper to taste

CHEESE SAUCE

Melt butter and stir in flour until smooth. Add milk and boil, stirring all the time until sauce thickens. Add remaining ingredients (reserving Parmesan cheese for topping). Pour over crepes. Sprinkle with Parmesan cheese and bake in moderate oven (350°) until lightly brown on top, approximately 20 minutes.

SAUCE

2 ounces butter
3 tablespoons flour
1 1/4 cups milk
1 cup grated cheddar cheese
1 tablespoon grated Parmesan cheese
1/2 teaspoon prepared mustard
onion salt and pepper to taste

POTATO PATTIES

2 pounds potatoes, sliced and
    peeled
2 eggs
2 ounces butter
2 tablespoons bread crumbs
onion salt and pepper to taste

Boil sliced potatoes until tender; drain. Mash with butter, eggs, onion salt, and pepper until very smooth. Refrigerate for one hour. Shape into patties, coat with crumbs, and place on greased cookie sheet. Bake for 20 minutes in 400° oven or until lightly brown; turn, baking other side until lightly brown also.

RICE SOUFFLE PUDDING

1 cup rice
2 cups milk
2 eggs, separated
3 tablespoons brown sugar
1 tablespoon honey
1 ounce butter
2 teaspoons vanilla
1 teaspoon grated lemon peel
1 teaspoon grated orange peel
1/2 cup seedless raisins
1 pint heavy cream, whipped

Cook rice in milk until very tender and milk is absorbed. Beat butter, sugar, and egg yolks until creamy and mix with cooked rice. Beat whites of eggs until stiff and fold into rice mixture. Add vanilla, raisins, orange and lemon peel, honey and mix. Place in buttered oven-proof dish and bake in moderate oven (375°) for about 20 minutes or until light brown. Cover with fruit glaze and serve warm or cold with whipped cream.

FRUIT GLAZE

1 1/2 cups raspberries
1 cup Dubonnet
3 ounces sugar
1/2 cup water
1 teaspoon cornstarch
1/2 teaspoon red vegetable coloring

Add Dubonnet to water and boil with berries and sugar for 15 minutes. Strain. Mix cornstarch with 1 tablespoon of water and add to strained sauce. Add red food color. Boil up once more, stirring all the time until smooth and clear. Spread over rice pudding.

MENU 7

ARTICHOKES WITH SPINACH-
YOGURT SAUCE
BAKED AVOCADO STUFFED
WITH BRAZIL NUTS
WINE SAUCE
ASPARAGUS
BLUEBERRY CREAM CHEESE PIE

All items in this menu can be prepared ahead of time except the stuffed avocado dish. This will taste better if baked no sooner than you need it. The filling can be prepared a few hours before, but avocados get too soft and discolored if cut too soon.

HELPFUL HINT

When it comes to slicing the blueberry cream cheese pie, have a bowl of boiling water handy and dip your knife before cutting each slice. This will give you a neater, cleaner-looking piece of pie. Moreover, if the pie is made the day before, it will cut more easily.

ARTICHOKES WITH SPINACH-YOGURT SAUCE

Boil artichokes in water with butter, onion salt, and pepper after snipping off prickly ends and rubbing them with lemon juice. Remove stems. Simmer slowly for 30 minutes, drain, and serve on individual plates with spinach-yogurt sauce.

Melt butter, fry sesame seeds till golden. Combine with rest of sauce ingredients and mix well. Refrigerate for at least 1 hour.

4 artichokes
2 cups water
2 tablespoons butter
juice of 1 lemon
onion salt and pepper

SAUCE
1/2 ounce butter
2 tablespoons sesame seed
1 8-ounce carton plain yogurt
1/2 cup fresh spinach, finely chopped
1/4 cup green onions, finely chopped
1/4 teaspoon dry mustard
onion salt and pepper

BAKED AVOCADO STUFFED WITH BRAZIL NUTS

Peel and cut avocados in lengthwise halves, removing stone. Rub with lemon juice and sprinkle a little onion salt and pepper over them. Place on buttered ovenproof dish. Mix finely ground nuts with Vermouth, egg, tomato, chives, grated cheese, onion salt, and pepper. Fill avocado halves and bake uncovered in preheated 450° oven for 15 minutes. Avocado tastes best if not cooked too long. Serve with wine sauce.

4 avocados
juice of 1 lemon
3/4 cup Brazil nuts, finely ground
2 tablespoons chives, finely chopped
1/4 cup Vermouth
1 egg
1/2 cup grated cheddar cheese
1 tomato, peeled and chopped
onion salt and pepper to taste

WINE SAUCE

Melt margarine, add flour, and stir until smooth. Add water and Vermouth and boil until sauce thickens, stirring all the time. Add Savita, Washington Broth, parsley, onion salt, and pepper and mix well. Serve over avocados.

2 ounces margarine
2 tablespoons flour
1/2 cup Vermouth
1 cup water
1/2 teaspoon Savita
1 teaspoon chopped parsley
1 package chicken-flavored Washington Broth
onion salt and pepper to taste

ASPARAGUS

2 pounds asparagus
1 ounce melted butter
onion salt and pepper to taste

Divide asparagus into four equal bundles and tie string around each; this will enable you to serve them without breaking. Place bundles in shallow covered pan with a little water. Simmer for 15 minutes, or until just tender. Remove excess water and pour melted butter over them, also adding a little onion salt and pepper.

BLUEBERRY CREAM CHEESE PIE

CRUST:
1 cup graham cracker crumbs
1/4 cup sugar
4 ounces melted butter

Mix all ingredients well and line pie plate. Bake in moderate (350°) oven for 5 minutes. Set aside.

FILLING:
1/2 cup sugar
1 8-ounce package cream cheese,
     softened at room temperature
1 teaspoon grated lemon peel
1 teaspoon vanilla
1 cup sour cream
1 can blueberry pie filling, or
2 cups fresh blueberries, cooked,
     and juice thickened with 1 table-
     spoon cornstarch

Blend sour cream, softened cream cheese, vanilla, grated lemon peel, and sugar. Mix very well and pour over blueberry mixture which has been placed into cooled crust. Bake for 15 minutes in 400° oven. Serve cold.

MENU 8

ORIENTAL SPINACH SALAD
WITH CROUTONS
CAULIFLOWER AU GRATIN
WITH MUSHROOMS AND GRAPES
STUFFED TOMATOES
CHOCOLATE TRUFFLE BALLS WITH
PINEAPPLE CHUNKS AND CREAM

The oriental spinach salad is more work than an ordinary tossed salad but it is well worth the trouble. The salad can be prepared in layers ahead of time, but save the dressing until half an hour before serving. Remember, you do not toss this salad.

HELPFUL HINT
If you feel a bit tired while preparing a special meal, boil a cup of water and stir in $3/4$ teaspoon of Savita (see General Information section). This makes a tasty drink and helps to give you that needed lift.

ORIENTAL SPINACH SALAD WITH CROUTONS

Make dressing by stirring oil into vinegar. Add ketchup, sugar, lemon juice, a little onion salt, and paprika. Mix well and set aside.

Thoroughly wash and dry the spinach. Tear into small pieces, forming bed in salad bowl. Thinly slice water chestnuts and place alternate layers of chestnuts, bamboo shoots, and bean sprouts on bed of spinach. Pour dressing over all, but do not toss. Sprinkle riced hard-boiled egg and toasted sesame seeds over top of salad and allow to marinate for ½ hour before serving. Serve with garlic croutons: cut toasted bread slices into cubes, not using crusts; melt butter in frying pan and quickly toss cubes in butter adding a little garlic salt.

½ cup salad oil
3 tablespoons tarragon vinegar
¼ cup ketchup
¼ cup granulated sugar
1 tablespoon lemon juice
½ pound fresh spinach
1 small can bamboo shoots
1 small can water chestnuts
¼ pound fresh bean sprouts
1 hard-boiled egg, riced
2 tablespoons toasted sesame seeds
2 cups toasted bread cubes
1 ounce butter
garlic salt
onion salt and paprika to taste

CAULIFLOWER AU GRATIN WITH MUSHROOMS AND GRAPES

Cook cauliflower in a little boiling water until barely cooked. Drain and set aside. Melt 1 ounce of the butter, fry mushrooms and set aside. Make cheese sauce by melting 2 ounces butter, adding flour and stirring smooth. Add milk. Bring to boil, stirring all the time until sauce thickens. Take off stove and add grated cheddar cheese, mustard, onion salt, pepper, and parsley, and mix until all is blended and cheese melted. Break cooked cauliflower into bite-sized pieces and place in buttered casserole dish. Sprinkle grapes and fried mushrooms over cauliflower. Cover all with sauce and sprinkle with Parmesan cheese. Before serving, broil or bake until brown on top. Serve with stuffed tomatoes.

1 cauliflower
1 cup sliced fresh mushrooms
3 ounces butter
2 tablespoons flour
1½ cups milk
1 cup grated cheddar cheese
½ teaspoon French mustard
½ cup chopped parsley
onion salt and pepper to taste
1 cup seedless grapes
½ cup grated Parmesan cheese

STUFFED TOMATOES

4 large tomatoes
4 small eggs
2 tablespoons chopped parsley
onion salt and pepper to taste

Slice off tops of tomatoes and scoop out insides. Fill with unbeaten raw egg, one to each tomato. Sprinkle with onion salt, pepper, and parsley and bake in buttered dish until eggs are set—400° for approximately 15 minutes.

CHOCOLATE TRUFFLE BALLS, PINEAPPLE CHUNKS, AND CREAM

10 ounces sweet chocolate
3/4 cup whipping cream
1/3 cup margarine
1 1/2 teaspoons kirsch
3/4 cup chocolate Decorettes
1 pineapple
1/2 teaspoon vanilla
1 teaspoon granulated sugar

Place chocolate in saucepan and slowly heat with 1/4 cup cream. Stir until chocolate is melted. Remove from heat. Melt margarine, add to chocolate, and mix well. Add kirsch and mix again. Chill in refrigerator for 1 hour, until mixture is firm enough to be rolled into small balls. Place chocolate Decorettes in small dish and roll balls in it until all are coated. Place in refrigerator until serving time. Prepare pineapple in bite-sized chunks. Whip remaining 1/2 cup cream, adding sugar and vanilla. Serve truffle balls and pineapple chunks on toothpicks and place cream in center bowl so that it can be used for dunking.

MENU 9

STUFFED CELERY PIECES
EGG AND MUSHROOM RISSOLES
CREAMED TURNIPS
BAKED POTATO DUMPLINGS
TOSSED SALAD WITH HONEY DRESSING
BRANDY-CHEESE CAKE

The dessert for this meal will be easier to handle if you can find the time to bake it the day before. The rest of the dinner will not take more than an hour to prepare, assuming that you have all the ingredients in the house and if a friend does not keep you on the telephone during preparation time.

HELPFUL HINT
If you are wondering what kind of wine to serve with a gourmet vegetarian meal, the answer is, suit your taste entirely. Personally, I always keep it on the light side. There are some very delicious pure fruit wines, other than grape wines, on the market, but if you have a favorite of your own, use it by all means.

STUFFED CELERY PIECES

Mash softened cream cheese with chives, caraway seed, onion salt. Stuff celery pieces and sprinkle with paprika. Serve on shredded lettuce.

1 8-ounce package cream cheese
1/2 cup chopped chives
1/2 teaspoon caraway seed
onion salt and paprika
1 head shredded lettuce
2 celery stalks, cut into 2-inch pieces

EGG AND MUSHROOM RISSOLES

Fry mushrooms and onions in margarine until brown. Mash hard-boiled eggs very fine with mayonnaise. Add to fried mushrooms and onions. Add dry mustard, Savita, parsley, chopped tomato, one raw egg, soya flour, onion salt, and pepper. Mix well and shape into rissoles. Dip in raw egg and then coat with bread crumbs. Fry in oil on all sides until golden brown.

1 cup fresh mushrooms, chopped very fine
1 cup chopped onion
1 ounce margarine
4 hard-boiled plus 2 raw eggs
2 tablespoons mayonnaise
1 teaspoon dry mustard
1/2 teaspoon Savita
2 tablespoons chopped parsley
1 tomato, peeled and chopped
3/4 cup soya flour
onion salt and pepper
1 cup bread crumbs
1 cup oil

CREAMED TURNIPS

Wash and peel turnips and chop up green leaves. Slice turnips. Boil in 1 1/2 cups water until tender, about 20 minutes. Drain but save water. Melt butter, add flour, stir until smooth. Add 1 1/4 cups of the drained turnip water and boil, stirring, until mixture thickens. Add turnips, chopped greens, Washington Broth, onion salt, and pepper and heat through.

2 pounds turnips, complete with green leaves
2 ounces butter
2 tablespoons flour
1 1/2 cups water
1 package chicken-flavored Washington Broth
onion salt and pepper to taste

BAKED POTATO DUMPLINGS

Boil potatoes until tender. Drain. Mash with butter until very fine and smooth. Add chopped chives, onion salt, pepper and raw egg. Refrigerate for 30 minutes. Shape into balls and place on buttered ovenproof plate. Bake in moderate (350°) oven for 30 minutes, until light brown.

6 potatoes, peeled and sliced
1 1/2 ounces butter
1 egg
1/2 cup chopped chives
onion salt and pepper to taste

GREEN TOSSED SALAD WITH HONEY DRESSING

2 teaspoons honey
1 teaspoon ketchup
½ cup mayonnaise
1 tablespoon grated Parmesan
   cheese
onion salt and pepper to taste
1 head lettuce

Mix first 5 ingredients and pour over shredded lettuce.

BRANDY-CHEESE CAKE

2 ounces butter
1 cup graham cracker crumbs
3 8-ounce packages cream cheese
1 cup granulated sugar
1 teaspoon lemon juice
1 teaspoon vanilla extract
4 eggs
1 teaspoon kirsch
3 tablespoons red currant jelly

Butter sides and bottom of spring-form cake pan and sprinkle with graham cracker crumbs. In mixer, beat softened cream cheese, sugar, lemon juice, vanilla, eggs, kirsch. When completely smooth, pour into prepared cake pan and bake in moderate oven (350°) about 40 minutes or until brown on top. Turn off oven and leave in for another few minutes. Take out and cool. Melt red currant jelly, heating it until dissolved. When slightly cooled, spread over top of cheese cake. It will solidify again on the cake, forming a topping.

MENU 10

AVOCADO GELATIN SALAD
WITH LEMON DRESSING
STUFFED EGGPLANT WITH WINE SAUCE
ROASTED POTATOES
MERINGUES WITH
CHOCOLATE MINT SAUCE

All gelatin salads are better if prepared the day before. The secret of spending as little time as possible on the preparation of a meal is to make sure that you have all ingredients conveniently available.

HELPFUL HINT

If you want to use placecards for your dinner company, make them earthy and natural by using washed large pebbles. Write or paint the names and any little additional design you wish to add. If you do not have the pebbles in your garden, you will find them at most garden supply stores.

AVOCADO GELATIN SALAD WITH LEMON DRESSING

Dissolve lime gelatin dessert in 2 cups boiling water. Add 1½ cups cold water. Chill until slightly congealed. Add mayonnaise and mix in electric mixer until well blended. Add diced avocado, walnuts, celery, peppers, onion salt, and pepper. Mix gently and refrigerate in square dish. When set, cut into squares and serve on shredded lettuce with lemon dressing.

2 3-ounce packages lime gelatin dessert
2 cups boiling water
1½ cups cold water
1 cup mayonnaise
1 cup diced avocado, mixed with juice of 1 lemon
½ cup chopped walnuts
1 head lettuce
½ cup chopped red peppers
½ cup chopped celery
onion salt and pepper to taste

To make the dressing, mix all the ingredients thoroughly and serve with avocado gelatin.

LEMON DRESSING
½ cup mayonnaise
juice of 1 lemon
1 teaspoon dill weed
1 tablespoon honey

STUFFED EGGPLANT WITH WINE SAUCE

Remove center core of eggplant, wash and dry. Make stuffing by mixing ground nuts, chopped onion, chopped tomato, grated cheese, parsley, egg, onion salt, and pepper. Mix well and stuff eggplant. Place in ovenproof dish and dot with margarine. Add ½ cup water and bake uncovered in moderate oven (350°) for 30 minutes or until stuffing looks brown at the edges and eggplant feels tender when fork-tested. Serve sliced, with the wine sauce.

1 large eggplant
½ cup finely ground Brazil nuts
½ cup chopped onion
1 chopped tomato
½ cup grated cheddar cheese
1 tablespoon chopped parsley
1 egg
1 ounce margarine
onion salt and pepper to taste

To make the sauce, fry vegetables in margarine for 5 minutes; add flour, 1 cup water, and the wine, stirring till it boils and thickens. Simmer for ten minutes, stirring, adding seasoning. Strain and serve with eggplant. If sauce is too thick, add a little more wine.

RED WINE SAUCE
1 chopped onion
1 sliced carrot
½ cup chopped celery
2 teaspoons chopped chives
2 ounces margarine
2 tablespoons flour
1 bay leaf
1 cup water
½ cup red wine
onion salt and pepper to taste

ROASTED POTATOES

6 large potatoes
2 ounces butter
1 tablespoon chopped parsley
onion salt and pepper

Peel potatoes and cut into chunks. Place on ovenproof dish. Sprinkle with onion salt and pepper and dot with butter. Bake in moderate oven (350°) for 30 minutes or until light brown and tender. Remove to serving dish and sprinkle with parsley. This dish can be baked at the same time as the eggplant.

MERINGUES WITH CHOCOLATE MINT SAUCE

butter, enough to grease cookie
    sheet
4 egg whites
7 tablespoons granulated sugar
1 pint whipping cream
16 chocolate peppermint creams
1/2 teaspoon creme de menthe

Beat whites of egg until very stiff. Add 6$^{1}/_{3}$ tablespoons of sugar and continue beating. Form small shells with back of a teaspoon on buttered cookie sheet. Sprinkle with 1 teaspoon sugar and bake in slow oven (300°) until light brown and dry. Cool. Fill with 1/2 pint of cream that has been whipped with 1 teaspoon sugar.

Make chocolate mint sauce by placing remaining unwhipped cream in saucepan; add creme de menthe and chocolate peppermint creams. Heat slowly until mints have been completely melted and sauce is smooth and warm. Serve over meringues.

MENU 11

RAW VEGETABLES WITH DIP
COTTAGE CHEESE BURGERS
GREEN PEPPER SAUCE
ORANGE BEETS
LEMON FINALE
WITH STRAWBERRY SAUCE

In this age of calorie-conscious people, the raw vegetable dip is always very popular. If you wish to garnish the cottage cheese burger platter and feel more ambitious than just plain parsley, why not try making cucumber spirals? They look appealing and are tasty too. Use a large cucumber (the imported long variety is best because it has fewer seeds), and cut it into 2-inch-long pieces. Starting with the skin cut a ⅛-inch-thick continuous spiral on each piece until you reach the seeds. Roll up and slice thinly.

HELPFUL HINT

Get more wear out of your rubber gloves. I am talking about the gloves most of us wear for cleaning and for kitchen chores. Somehow, we always get left with too many left-hand gloves because the right-hand glove wears out first. Instead of throwing out the leftover good gloves, turn them inside out to make a right-hand glove. Your two hands may not match in color, but you will certainly get more wear out of your investment.

RAW VEGETABLES WITH DIP

Make dip by mixing sour cream with mustard, dill, onion salt, and pepper. Cut up vegetables into bite-sized pieces and put on toothpicks.

2 small zucchinis
2 cups cauliflower, in bite-sized
  pieces
6 radishes
6 carrot strips
1 cup sour cream
2 teaspoons mustard
1 teaspoon dill weed, chopped fine
onion salt and pepper to taste
toothpicks

COTTAGE CHEESE BURGERS

Mix cottage cheese with chives, soya flour, onion salt, dash sugar, pepper and one egg. Mix well and shape into burgers. Dip into remaining beaten eggs and coat with bread crumbs. Heat oil and brown burgers on all sides quickly. Speed is important so cottage cheese does not melt too much. Drain on paper towel.

1½ cups small curd cottage cheese
¾ cup soya flour
3 eggs
1 cup chopped chives
1 cup bread crumbs
1 cup oil
onion salt and pepper to taste
dash sugar

GREEN PEPPER SAUCE

Add flour to melted butter and stir over heat until smooth. Add milk and bring to boil, stirring all the time until sauce thickens. Add chopped peppers and boil very slowly for 5 minutes, stirring to avoid sticking. Add seasoning and serve on burgers.

2 ounces butter
2 tablespoons flour
1¼ cups milk
1 cup finely chopped green peppers
1 package chicken-flavored Washington Broth
onion salt and pepper to taste

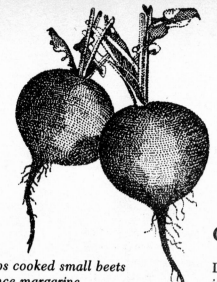

ORANGE BEETS

3 cups cooked small beets
1 ounce margarine
¼ cup orange juice
¼ cup honey
1 tablespoon lemon juice
1 tablespoon brown sugar
1 tablespoon cornstarch

Drain beets and toss them with melted margarine. Add juices, honey, and sugar. Mix cornstarch in separate bowl with just enough cold water to form a paste. Add to beets. Boil up again briefly, stirring all the time gently until mixture thickens. Marinate for an hour before reheating for dinner.

LEMON FINALE

4 ounces butter
4 tablespoons flour
1 cup milk
1 cup granulated sugar
3 eggs, separated
juice of 3 lemons
grated lemon peel

Add flour to melted butter and stir until smooth. Add milk and bring to boil, stirring all the time until mixture thickens. Away from stove, add egg yolks, lemon juice, and some grated lemon rind and sugar. Finally, add egg whites, stiffly beaten. Mix all gently and bake in greased ovenproof dish in 350° oven for about 25 minutes or until very lightly browned. Serve warm with strawberry sauce.

STRAWBERRY SAUCE

2 cups fresh strawberries or
10-ounce package frozen strawber-
ries
1 cup berry wine (if frozen berries
are used, use only ½ cup wine)
½ cup sugar
1 tablespoon cornstarch
1 tablespoon lemon juice
¼ teaspoon red vegetable food
coloring

Boil berries in wine, lemon juice, and sugar for 15 minutes. Pass through strainer or put in blender. Cool a little. Mix cornstarch with a little of the fruit juice, add paste to remaining sauce, and boil up again, stirring until mixture thickens. Add the food coloring if needed. Serve cold over lemon finale.

MENU 12

VICHYSSOISE
STUFFED FRENCH ROLLS
MIXED SALAD
RAW APPLE DELIGHT

This menu is best suited to a summer meal because of the cold soup. It is a most tasty combination and popular with young and old alike.

HELPFUL HINT

Here is a centerpiece for your dinner table that is not in my special chapter on table decorations but is fun to make and will last you a long time. Use an over-sized champagne glass and plant a little terrarium. I am sure you can find two or three cuttings in your garden or in a friend's garden. Ivy, strawberry, or miniature ferns and palm trees are very suitable. Be sure to keep sides of glass clean while planting. Use small rocks underneath the planting mix to allow for water drainage. This centerpiece will last you a lot longer than your meal.

VICHYSSOISE

Melt margarine in soup kettle and fry leeks and chopped onion for a few minutes. Add sliced potatoes, water, Washington Broth, garlic flakes, curry powder, dry mustard, onion salt, and pepper, and simmer for 30 minutes, covered. Press through sieve or puree in blender. Return to stove to heat again, adding milk. Cool in refrigerator. Before serving, blend thoroughly (soup should be very smooth) and mix with cream and chives. Serve cold.

2 ounces margarine
3 sliced leeks
1 chopped onion
5 large potatoes, peeled and sliced
2¹/₂ cups water
2 packages chicken-flavored Washington Broth
¹/₂ teaspoon curry powder
¹/₄ teaspoon garlic flakes
¹/₄ teaspoon dry mustard
1 cup milk
¹/₂ cup cream
4 tablespoons chopped chives
onion salt and pepper to taste

STUFFED FRENCH ROLLS

Heat rolls on cookie sheet in 350° oven for 5 minutes and then cool. Mix remaining ingredients thoroughly. Slice tops off rolls about 1 inch down from one end. Remove most of the soft insides of rolls. Fill with cheese mixture and replace top. Wrap each roll tightly in aluminum foil, turning up ends of foil to make an air-tight package. Before serving, heat foil packages on cookie sheet for 20 minutes in 400° oven. Serve hot with mixed salad.

8 French rolls
2 cups grated cheddar cheese
6 tablespoons ketchup
¹/₂ cup chopped green onions
¹/₂ teaspoon French mustard
¹/₂ cup pitted and chopped black olives
onion salt and pepper to taste
aluminum foil

MIXED SALAD

1 head Boston lettuce
12 spinach leaves
1 tomato
½ cup zucchini, thinly sliced
½ cup very thin red onion rings
1 teaspoon dill weed
1 cup watercress
⅓ cup salad oil
8 tablespoons vinegar
onion salt, pepper, and sugar to
    taste
½ cup toasted sesame seeds
2 egg yolks, hard-boiled

Wash, dry, and shred lettuce into salad bowl. Add coarsely chopped spinach leaves, sliced and peeled tomato (pouring boiling water over tomato for half a minute makes it easy to peel), zucchini slices, red onion rings, watercress, and dill weed. Make French dressing by mixing oil with vinegar, onion salt, pepper and pinch of sugar. Pour over salad and decorate with toasted sesame seed and riced egg yolk.

RAW APPLE DELIGHT

3 eating apples
juice of 1 lemon
1 tablespoon oatmeal
3 tablespoons orange juice
2 tablespoons heavy cream
1 tablespoon grated orange rind
3 tablespoons brown sugar
2 teaspoons honey
6 tablespoons finely ground al-
    monds

Soak oatmeal for 8 hours in orange juice. Wash and grate apples with skin and add lemon juice to prevent discoloration. Mix cream with oats (which have soaked up the orange juice) and add to apples together with orange rind, brown sugar, honey. Mix in ground nuts and chill in covered dish.

MENU 13

POTATO AND LEEK SOUP
LENTIL ROAST
TOMATO SAUCE
SESAME POTATO BALLS
CABBAGE WITH CARAWAY SEED
APPLE SAUCE WITH MACAROONS

In contrast to Menu 12, this dinner is a good cold-weather meal, although it does not have to be limited to winter months.

HELPFUL HINT

If this has been a messy kitchen day, you will appreciate this easy method of oven cleaning. (I am talking to those of you who are not fortunate enough to own a self-cleaning oven.) To remove burned food or food droppings from your oven, saturate a small cloth with ammonia and place in oven overnight, closing oven door. Next morning you will find it very easy to remove sticky spots.

POTATO LEEK SOUP

Cook sliced potatoes and leeks in melted margarine for 5 minutes. Add 5 cups of water, Savita, Washington Broth, cream, onion salt, and pepper. Boil slowly for 1 hour. Strain and serve with parmesan cheese.

3 sliced potatoes
2 sliced leeks
2 ounces margarine
2 packages chicken-flavored Washington Broth
1 teaspoon Savita
5 cups water
onion salt and pepper to taste
2 tablespoons light cream
1/2 cup grated Parmesan cheese

LENTIL ROAST

Soak lentils for a couple of hours in hot water and then boil in same water until tender—about 1/2 hour. Drain. Mix lentils with grated cheese, ketchup, Savita, eggs, parsley, onion salt, and pepper. Pour into well-greased flat baking pan and bake in moderate oven (350°) for about 30 minutes or until light brown on top. Cut into squares and serve with tomato sauce.

1 cup lentils
1 cup grated cheddar cheese
2 teaspoons ketchup
3 eggs
2 tablespoons chopped parsley
1/2 teaspoon Savita
1 ounce margarine to grease pan
onion salt and pepper to taste

TOMATO SAUCE

Cut up tomatoes and cook with chopped onion in melted margarine. After 5 minutes add oregano, 1/2 cup water, ketchup, and seasoning. Boil slowly for 15 minutes. Strain and serve with lentil roast.

4 tomatoes
1 chopped onion
1 ounce margarine
1/2 cup water
1 teaspoon ketchup
1/2 teaspoon oregano
onion salt, pepper, and sugar to taste

SESAME POTATO BALLS

Boil potatoes until tender, and drain. Mash with fork, adding 1 ounce butter, egg, onion salt, and pepper. Refrigerate for 30 minutes. Form into small balls and roll in sesame seed. Place on greased cookie sheet using remaining 1/2 ounce butter and bake for 20 minutes or until brown.

5 large potatoes
1 1/2 ounces butter
1 egg
onion salt and pepper to taste
1/2 cup sesame seeds

CABBAGE WITH CARAWAY SEED

1 head green cabbage
1 teaspoon caraway seed
1½ ounces butter
½ cup water
onion salt and pepper to taste

Shred cabbage and cook in melted butter with caraway seed, onion salt, and pepper. After 5 minutes, add ½ cup water. Simmer for another 5 minutes.

APPLESAUCE

6 large green cooking apples
1 cup water
1 slice lemon
½ cup brown sugar

Peel, core, and quarter apples. Boil with 1 cup water, lemon slice, and sugar. Cook covered over low heat for 15 minutes. Cool and serve with macaroons.

MACAROONS

2 egg whites
12 tablespoons finely ground al-
    monds
12 tablespoons granulated sugar
½ teaspoon almond extract
½ ounce margarine to grease cook-
    ie sheet

Beat egg whites until very stiff. Add ground almonds, sugar, and almond extract. Drop in teaspoonsful on greased cookie sheet and shape macaroons with back tip of teaspoon. Bake in moderate (350°) oven for about 20 minutes until light brown. Do not overbake.

MENU 14

VEGETABLE-NOODLE SOUP
PROTEIN-STUFFED ZUCCHINI HALVES
BROILED MUSHROOMS
CREAMED SPINACH
COFFEE-STRAWBERRY SPONGE

This meal is sufficiently elegant to serve to any company.

HELPFUL HINT

How about serving champagne cocktails before the meal? Prepare champagne glasses by dipping top of glasses in ice water, immersing ⅛ inch (a saucer filled with ice water will do nicely), and immediately dip edge of glass in fine granulated sugar on another saucer. Be sure to let the sugar harden in the upside-down position so that it does not run down the side of the glass. When glasses are dry, turn right-side-up and place 1 sugar cube in bottom of each glass. Saturate with 3 drops of Angostura aromatic bitters. Add 1 teaspoon of any brandy, and fill remainder of glasses with champagne. Serving champagne this way is always a winner.

VEGETABLE-NOODLE SOUP

Wash vegetables and cut up into fairly small pieces. Cook in melted margarine for a few minutes. Add 5 cups of water, Savita, Washington Broth, onion salt, pepper, and a pinch of sugar. Boil up and then simmer for 1 hour. Strain, pressing most of the pulp through sieve or use blender. Add cooked noodles.

2 onions
1 leek
1 celery stalk
1 carrot
1 cup cauliflower, bite-sized pieces
2 ounces margarine
5 cups water
¼ cup chopped parsley
1 teaspoon Savita
3 packages chicken-flavored Washington Broth
1 cup cooked noodles
onion salt, pepper, sugar to taste

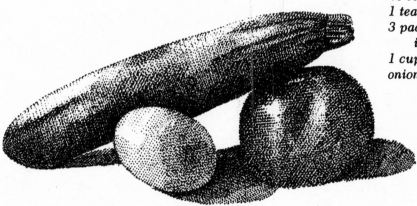

PROTEIN-STUFFED ZUCCHINI HALVES

Cut zucchinis in halves and remove seeds (seeds may be used in stuffing). Mix seeds with remaining ingredients except margarine, and stuff zucchinis. Add ½ inch water to casserole and fill with stuffed zucchinis. Place a few dabs of margarine on top and bake in moderate oven (350°) for approximately 30 minutes until cooked and lightly browned.

8 zucchinis (about 4 inches long)
½ cup finely ground Brazil nuts
½ cup grated swiss cheese
1 tomato, chopped (without skin and seeds)
1 ounce margarine
1 egg
onion salt and pepper to taste

BROILED MUSHROOMS

Wash and dry mushrooms after removing stems. Make a basting solution by mixing the remaining ingredients. Place mushroom caps on broiling pan and brush with basting solution. Broil until cooked and lightly browned. Turn and baste and broil other side very briefly.

16 large mushrooms
½ cup oil
3 teaspoons tarragon vinegar
¼ teaspoon garlic salt

CREAMED SPINACH

2 pounds fresh spinach
³/₄ cup water
1 chopped onion
1¹/₂ ounces margarine
2 level tablespoons flour
1 package chicken-flavored Washington Broth
onion salt and pepper to taste

Wash spinach leaves and simmer in ³/₄ cup water for 5 minutes. Drain, retaining water in separate dish. Fry chopped onion in the margarine. When golden, add flour and stir until smooth. Add spinach water to onion mixture and boil briefly, stirring all the time. Add drained chopped spinach, Washington Broth, onion salt, and pepper.

COFFEE-STRAWBERRY SPONGE

3 eggs, separated
4 tablespoons granulated sugar plus 1 teaspoon for whipped cream
3 tablespoons flour
2 cups sliced strawberries
1 cup red currant jelly
¹/₄ cup plus 1 tablespoon water
1 teaspoon cornstarch
¹/₂ pint whipping cream
1 teaspoon instant coffee
¹/₂ cup chocolate curls shaved off sweet chocolate bar with sharp knife or vegetable parer

Use ungreased spring-form cake pan. Make sponge by beating 3 tablespoons of the sugar with egg yolks until lemon colored. Fold in stiffly beaten whites and flour. Bake in moderate oven (325°) for 15 to 20 minutes until very lightly browned. Cool. Meanwhile wash and slice berries and sprinkle 1 tablespoon of sugar over them. Spread over cooled sponge. Melt red currant jelly in saucepan with ¹/₄ cup water. Mix cornstarch with 1 tablepoon water and add to jelly. Boil, stirring all the time until thickened and clear. Spoon over berries until all are covered. Cool. Whip cream and add 1 teaspoon sugar and instant coffee. When stiff (test if sweet enough) spread over cold berries and decorate with chocolate curls. Refrigerate until serving time.

MENU 15

FRESH ORANGE SALAD
MUSHROOM RICE
EGGS IN SAUCE
SWEET AND SOUR RED CABBAGE
PEACH CRISP

If you aspire to becoming a gourmet vegetarian cook, this dinner will help you achieve your goal. People may not eat as much today as they used to, but they surely think more about the value of foods. Your efforts will therefore be appreciated.

HELPFUL HINT

When you wax your floors, wax the bottoms of your chairs too. This will prevent them from scratching the shiny floors.

FRESH ORANGE SALAD

Cut each orange, including peel, into 6 lengthwise sections, avoiding center core. Use serrated knife and remove orange sections from peel. Add sugar and honey to orange sections. Serve in individual dishes, sprinkled with toasted shredded coconut.

4 large oranges
2 tablespoons brown sugar
2 teaspoons honey
1/2 cup toasted shredded coconut

MUSHROOM RICE

Boil rice until tender and drain. Fry chopped onion and mushrooms in melted margarine. Add fried vegetables, parsley, Washington Broth, onion salt, and pepper to rice.

2 cups brown rice
2 ounces margarine
1 cup fresh sliced mushrooms
1/2 cup chopped onion
1/2 cup chopped parsley
1 package chicken-flavored Washington Broth
onion salt and pepper to taste

EGGS IN SAUCE

Cut eggs into slices with egg cutter. Make sauce by frying peppers in melted margarine; add flour, and stir until smooth before adding milk. Bring to boil, stirring all the time until sauce thickens. Add remaining ingredients and mix well. Add eggs last and serve over rice.

6 hard-boiled eggs
4 ounces margarine
3 tablespoons flour
1/2 cup chopped green peppers
1 1/2 cups milk
1 package chicken-flavored Washington Broth
1/2 teaspoon Savita
1/4 cup chopped chives

SWEET AND SOUR
RED CABBAGE

Shred red cabbage and fry with chopped onions in butter for 5 minutes. Add lemon juice, sugar, and water. Boil slowly for 1 hour. Season to taste.

1 medium-sized red cabbage
2 ounces butter
1/2 cup chopped onion
juice of 2 lemons
2 cups water
2 tablespoons brown sugar
onion salt and pepper to taste

PEACH CRISP

8 firm peaches
¼ cup granulated sugar
1 teaspoon lemon juice
¾ cup flour
¾ cup brown sugar
¼ pound butter
½ cup chopped walnuts

Peel, pit, and slice peaches into pie dish. Mix lemon juice with granulated sugar and pour over peaches. In a separate bowl combine flour, brown sugar, and nuts. Melt butter and pour over flour mixture and mix with fork, making crumbs. Sprinkle over peaches and bake in moderate oven (350°) for 30 minutes. (If fresh peaches are not available, canned fruit may be used without the juice.)

MENU 16

CARROT AND RAISIN SALAD
SOYBEAN SQUARES
WITH THYME SAUCE
EGGPLANT AND TOMATO ROUNDS
APPLE CHARLOTTE

If it seems too much to prepare the apple charlotte, save it for another day when you feel more ambitious. It is not hard to prepare but takes a little time. I know you and your family or guests will enjoy it whenever you serve it.

HELPFUL HINT

In the meantime, here is a very quick and easy dessert sauce. You can serve it over any fresh or stewed fruit. Soften an 8-ounce package of cream cheese and blend with ½ pint sour cream. Add a little granulated sugar and serve over fruit.

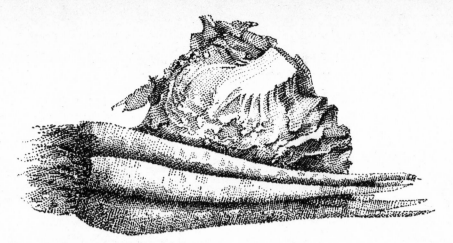

CARROT AND RAISIN SALAD

Pour boiling water over raisins and soak raisins in boiling water for 1/2 hour; drain. Grate carrots in bowl. Add drained raisins and mix in remaining ingredients. Marinate 1/2 hour before placing on lettuce beds on individual salad plates.

4 carrots
1/2 cup seedless raisins
2 tablespoons lemon juice
1 tablespoon brown sugar
1 teaspoon mayonnaise
1/4 teaspoon ground ginger
lettuce to form beds for salad

SOYBEAN SQUARES

Pour 3 cups boiling water over soybeans and soak for 1 hour. Using the same water in which the beans have been soaked, add the bay leaf and boil slowly for 3 hours or until tender, adding a little water from time to time if necessary. When tender, drain any excess liquid and reserve for sauce. Remove bay leaf. Mix beans with remaining ingredients and place in greased square oven-proof dish. Bake in moderate oven (350°) for 30 minutes until firm and brown. Cut into squares and serve with thyme sauce.

1 cup soybeans
1 bay leaf
1/2 cup tomato sauce
2 eggs
1 cup grated cauliflower
1 cup grated cheddar cheese
4 tablespoons soya flour
2 tablespoons chopped parsley
1/4 teaspoon savory
onion salt and pepper to taste
margarine for greasing dish

THYME SAUCE

Melt butter, add flour, and stir until smooth. Add milk and water and bring to boil, stirring all the time until sauce thickens. Add remaining ingredients.

2 ounces butter
2 tablespoons flour
1 cup milk
1/2 cup water, using that drained from beans if possible
1 teaspoon chopped fresh thyme or 1/2 teaspoon dried thyme
1 package chicken-flavored Washington Broth
onion salt and pepper to taste

EGGPLANT AND TOMATO ROUNDS

1 large eggplant, cut into 12 slices
¼ cup salad oil
1 teaspoon tarragon vinegar
¼ teaspoon garlic salt
1 teaspoon Italian seasoning
¼ teaspoon sugar
4 firm tomatoes
½ cup grated Parmesan cheese
onion salt and pepper to taste

Place eggplant slices on broiler pan. Mix oil, garlic salt, vinegar, Italian seasoning, sugar, onion salt, and pepper in a cup. Baste eggplant slices with this mixture. Broil for 3 to 4 minutes and turn. Baste other side and broil again briefly. Slice tomatoes and place one slice on each eggplant slice. Baste and sprinkle with Parmesan cheese. Broil until golden brown and serve hot with bean-squares.

APPLE CHARLOTTE

2 pounds green apples
4 tablespoons brown sugar
13 slices cinnamon-raisin bread
¼ teaspoon cinnamon
2 ounces butter
½ cup sherry

Butter pie plate and sprinkle with 2 tablespoons brown sugar. Melt remaining butter and dip the bread slices in, first removing crusts and cutting slices in half to make it easier to line pie plate. With dipped bread, line bottom and sides of pie plate, using buttered side to secure bread. Peel and core apples and cut into slices. Mix with remaining brown sugar, cinnamon, and sherry, and boil for 5 minutes. Then fill pie plate with this mixture. Cover apples with remaining bread slices, also removing crusts, cutting in half, and dipping in melted butter. Sprinkle top with a little more brown sugar and bake in moderate oven (350°) for 30 minutes. Turn out before serving, but serve warm.

MENU 17

BARLEY SOUP
ZUCCHINI AND SWISS CHEESE BAKE
BAKED BUTTERED POTATOES
GREEN BEAN SALAD
BROILED LEMON BANANAS

The criterion of a successful meal is not how good the individual dishes are but how much excitement the total menu produces. An element of surprise is always appreciated, and enthusiasm is contagious—try it on your family and friends. Zucchinis can be bought in the United States all year round, and this is a most versatile vegetable. The casserole described in this menu is very simple and delicious.

HELPFUL HINT
Keep a toothbrush (the soft variety) handy around your kitchen sink. It facilitates cleaning of rotary beaters, graters, and other kitchen utensils.

BARLEY SOUP

Clean and cut up vegetables and parsley and fry in butter until lightly browned. Add water, Savita and Washington Broth. Simmer for 45 minutes. Strain, pressing as many of the vegetables through strainer as you can, or put soup in blender. Add onion salt, pepper, and a little sugar to taste. Cook barley in boiling water until tender. Drain and add barley to soup.

3 onions
1 bunch celery
1 carrot
1 large potato
1 tomato
2 sprigs parsley
4 cups water
1½ ounces margarine
3 packages chicken-flavored Washington Broth
1 teaspoon Savita
onion salt, pepper, and sugar to taste

ZUCCHINI AND SWISS CHEESE BAKE

Butter ovenproof dish. Wash and slice zucchinis and put them in casserole. Scatter peeled cherry tomatoes over them. Dot with margarine over last layer of zucchini and add onion salt and pepper. Top with slices of Swiss cheese, over which you sprinkle the sage. Bake in moderate oven (350°) about 30 minutes until cheese topping is brown.

12 small zucchinis
12 peeled cherry tomatoes (pour boiling water over them for ½ minute before peeling)
8 slices Swiss cheese
½ teaspoon sage
1 ounce margarine
onion salt and pepper to taste

BAKED BUTTERED POTATOES

Butter ovenproof dish. Peel and slice potatoes and place in dish. Top with dabs of butter, onion salt, and pepper. Bake in oven (can be done the same time as the zucchinis) for about 45 minutes until tender and lightly browned. Before serving, sprinkle with parsley.

6 potatoes
1½ ounces butter
2 tablespoons chopped parsley
onion salt and pepper to taste

GREEN BEAN SALAD

1 pound green string beans
1/2 cup salad oil
2 tablespoons tarragon
    vinegar
1/2 cup lemon juice
1 teaspoon dry mustard
1 hard-boiled egg yolk
2 tablespoons capers
onion salt, pepper, sugar to taste

Wash and string beans, breaking off the ends. Cook in a little boiling water until tender, and drain. Combine oil, vinegar, lemon juice, onion salt, pepper, mustard, and a little sugar. Pour dressing over warm drained beans and mix lightly. Allow to marinate in refrigerator for 2 hours. Before serving, drain beans and arrange in neat bundles on individual salad plates. Decorate with capers and riced egg yolk.

BROILED LEMON BANANAS

6 firm bananas
1 ounce butter
juice of 1 lemon
2 tablespoons honey

Peel and slice bananas in halves. Place on buttered broiling pan. Melt butter and mix with lemon juice and honey. Spoon a little over each banana half and broil until golden brown.

MENU 18

DILL CUCUMBER SALAD
EGG AND OLIVE CROQUETTES
GREEN PEPPER SAUCE
BROCCOLI
NOODLES AU GRATIN
APRICOT-WINE CREAM

If you are a career woman, get home at 5:30 P.M., and expect company by 7 P.M., you can handle this dinner in 45 minutes or less, especially if you prepare the cucumber salad the evening before and have the apricots cooked and pureed ahead of time.

HELPFUL HINT

Since this dessert will leave an egg yolk for future use, here is the best way to store it. Put left-over egg yolks in a small jar and cover with a film of cold water. Cover the jar tightly and refrigerate. You should use these yolks within one or two days. They will be happy to join your scrambled eggs for breakfast.

DILL CUCUMBER SALAD

Wash and dry lettuce before placing on individual plates. In a bowl, slice cucumber very finely and marinate in French dressing made from oil, vinegar, onion salt, pepper, sugar and dill weed. Allow to marinate for ½ hour and drain before placing on lettuce.

1 cucumber
½ cup salad oil
¼ cup vinegar
1 teaspoon chopped dill weed
onion salt, pepper, sugar to taste
lettuce for salad beds

EGG AND OLIVE CROQUETTES

Melt margarine, add flour, and stir until smooth before adding milk. Bring to boil, stirring all the time, until mixture thickens. Allow to cool. Add chopped hard-cooked eggs, chopped olives, and seasonings, and mix well. Refrigerate for at least 1 hour and form croquettes. Beat raw eggs. Place bread crumbs in separate bowl. Dip croquettes into raw egg and then in bread crumbs until well coated, and fry in hot oil until golden on all sides. Drain on paper towel. Serve with green pepper sauce.

1½ ounces margarine
3 tablespoons flour
¾ cup milk
8 hard-boiled eggs, chopped
½ cup olives, pitted and chopped
½ teaspoon savory
¼ cup bread crumbs
2 raw eggs
1 cup oil
onion salt and pepper to taste

GREEN PEPPER SAUCE

Melt butter, add flour, and stir until smooth before adding milk. Boil, stirring all the time, until sauce thickens. Add grated cheese, peppers, onion salt, and pepper, and cook slowly for 5 minutes, stirring. Serve over croquettes.

2 ounces butter
2 tablespoons flour
1 cup milk
½ cup finely chopped green peppers
½ cup grated cheddar cheese
onion salt and pepper to taste

BROCCOLI

Wash broccoli and cut into long pieces. Boil in very little water until just tender. Drain excess liquid. Pour melted butter and seasoning over broccoli.

2 pounds fresh broccoli
½ ounce butter
onion salt and pepper

NOODLES AU GRATIN

4 cups vermicelli noodles
1¹/₂ ounces margarine
¹/₂ cup chopped parsley
1 cup grated Parmesan cheese
onion salt and pepper to taste

Cook noodles in boiling water until just tender. Drain. Melt margarine in saucepan and toss noddles in margarine. Add Parmesan cheese, parsley, onion salt, and pepper, and mix.

APRICOT-WINE CREAM

¹/₂ pound dried apricots
³/₄ cup granulated sugar
¹/₃ cup sweet sherry
1 cup heavy cream
1 egg white
¹/₄ cup almonds, toasted and slivered

Boil apricots until tender; drain and cool. Puree the apricots with the sherry by using blender or by pressing all the fruit through strainer. Beat egg white stiff, add sugar. Add to apricot mixture. Whip cream and add to mixture, reserving just a little for decorating. Decorate with remaining whipped cream and slivered almonds and serve chilled in individual glasses.

MENU 19

EGG DROP SOUP
NUT AND MUSHROOM GOULASH
FRIED CAULIFLOWER PIECES
POTATOES AU GRATIN
APPLE SOUFFLE

Menu 19 is a conversation piece. If you follow the instructions carefully, you will not find it hard to cook this meal. You do not have to worry about menu planning or balancing food values; just relax and ride along with me, making sure that you have all ingredients in the house before we start.

HELPFUL HINT

Here is the best way to keep cheese fresh. Moisten a piece of cheesecloth with white wine and wrap the cheese in the moistened cloth. Store wrapped cheese in a closed container in your refrigerator. If you are keeping the cheese for any length of time, replace the moistened cloth every few days.

EGG DROP SOUP

Melt margarine and fry chopped onions, chives, carrot, celery, and parsley for 5 minutes. Add water, Washington Broth, Savita, and seasonings. Boil slowly for 1 hour. Strain or blend in osterizer.

SOUP

2 large onions
1 cup chopped celery
1 carrot
2 sprigs parsley
2 tablespoons chopped chives
1 teaspoon Savita
6 cups water
4 packages chicken-flavored Washington Broth
1¹/₂ ounces margarine
onion salt, pepper, and a pinch of sugar

Mix all egg drop ingredients and place in refrigerator for 1 hour. Bring 6 cups of water to boil and drop ¹/₂ teaspoon of egg mixture into boiling water until all is used up. Simmer slowly for 15 minutes until all egg drops float on top. Drain and add to strained soup.

EGG DROPS

1 tablespoon melted margarine
1 egg
enough flour to make a soft paste (approximately 2 tablespoons)
1 tablespoon chopped parsley
onion salt and pepper to taste

NUT AND MUSHROOM GOULASH

Chop the onion and fry in melted margarine for a couple of minutes. Add sliced mushrooms and chopped green onions and cook for 3 or 4 minutes. Add flour and stir until smooth. Add 2 cups water and boil, stirring all the time. Add Savita, Washington Broth, onion salt, pepper, savory, and nuts. Cook and stir for 5 minutes. Finally, add sliced eggs.

1 small onion
2 ounces margarine
2 cups sliced mushrooms
2 chopped green onions
3 tablespoons flour
2 cups water
¹/₂ teaspoon Savita
1 package chicken-flavored Washington Broth
¹/₄ teaspoon savory
onion salt and pepper to taste
³/₄ cup Brazil nuts, cut into halves
2 hard-boiled eggs, sliced

FRIED CAULIFLOWER PIECES

1 medium-sized cauliflower
2 eggs
onion salt and pepper to taste
1 cup bread crumbs
1 cup oil

Wash cauliflower, dry, and cut into bite-sized pieces. Mix eggs, onion salt, and pepper. Dip cauliflower pieces into egg and then coat with bread crumbs. Fry in oil until brown on all sides and drain on paper towel.

POTATOES AU GRATIN

2 pounds potatoes
2 ounces butter (plus enough to butter dish)
1 chopped onion
2 tablespoons flour
1 cup milk
2 ounces grated Parmesan cheese
onion salt and pepper to taste
1 tablespoon bread crumbs

Steam potatoes in jackets until tender. Peel and cut into slices. Make a sauce by frying chopped onion in 2 ounces butter. Add flour and stir until smooth. Add milk and bring to boil, stirring until sauce thickens. Set aside. Butter ovenproof dish. Make layers of sliced potatoes, sprinkling each with onion salt, pepper, and Parmesan cheese. Repeat layers until all is used, finishing with a topping of sauce, Parmesan cheese, and bread crumbs. Bake in moderate oven (350°) for 20 minutes until light brown on top.

APPLE SOUFFLE

4 green apples
1 ounce butter
1 cup sugar
juice of 1 lemon
3 eggs, separated
1 teaspoon vanilla extract
1/2 cup sour cream
1/2 pint whipped cream

Peel and core apples and cut into slices. Melt butter in large pan. Add 2/3 cup of sugar, lemon juice, and apples. Cook over low heat until apples are tender and liquid is absorbed. Place apples in greased ovenproof dish. Beat egg whites until stiff, adding the last 1/3 cup of sugar. In a separate bowl beat yolks of eggs, vanilla, and sour cream. Fold into egg whites. Pour all over apples. Bake in medium oven for 20 minutes until souffle is puffed and browned. Serve warm or cold and pass the whipped cream in separate dish.

MENU 20

PAPAYA HALVES
CHEESE SOUFFLE
PARSLEY SAUCE
KALE
TOMATO SALAD
CHOCOLATE CREAMPUFFS

You will have discovered that many of my recipes call for the use of herbs. I hope that I have convinced you that they are indispensable aids to gourmet cooking.

You may never have eaten fresh kale before, and not all food markets carry it. However, I have never had a problem locating a store that does, and it is well worth the effort both from a nutritional point of view and as a taste experience.

HELPFUL HINT

Many people have asked me whether avocados contain cholesterol and starch. Avocados contain no cholesterol, which is mostly found in meats and eggs. The California Avocado Advisory Board tells us that avocados contain no starch.

PAPAYA HALVES

Cut papayas in halves and remove seeds. Mix lemon juice with sugar and sprinkle over papayas.

2 fresh papayas
juice of 1 lemon
1 tablespoon brown sugar

CHEESE SOUFFLE

Melt butter, add flour, and stir until smooth. Add milk, stirring vigorously until paste forms and leaves sides of saucepan. Allow to cool a little. Add grated cheese and yolks of eggs. Beat whites of eggs until stiff and fold into cheese mixture. Add chives, onion salt, and pepper. Bake at 375° in buttered ovenproof souffle dish for approximately 30 minutes, or until lightly brown on top and knife comes out clean when inserted into souffle. Serve with parsley sauce.

4 ounces butter
4 heaping tablespoons flour
1 cup milk
8 ounces grated cheddar cheese
5 eggs, separated
1/2 cup chopped chives
onion salt and pepper to taste

PARSLEY SAUCE

Melt butter, add flour, and stir until smooth. Add milk and bring to boil, stirring all the time until sauce thickens. Add parsley and seasonings. Serve over cheese souffle.

2 ounces butter
2 tablespoons flour
1 1/2 cups milk
1/2 cup chopped parsley
onion salt and pepper to taste

KALE

Chop up kale and boil in small amount of water until tender, about 30 minutes. Drain excess water and add margarine and seasoning.

2 pounds fresh kale
1/2 ounce margarine
onion salt and pepper to taste

TOMATO SALAD

Pour boiling water over tomatoes and allow to stand for 1 minute. Drain off water and peel tomatoes. Slice very thin and place on individual salad plates. Make French dressing by mixing remaining ingredients, and spoon over tomatoes.

6 firm, large tomatoes
1/2 cup oil
1/4 cup vinegar
1 teaspoon chopped dill weed
onion salt, pepper, and a pinch of
*   sugar*

CHOCOLATE CREAMPUFFS

¹/₄ pound butter + ¹/₂ ounce for
greasing
1 cup hot water
1 tablespoon granulated sugar
1 cup flour
4 eggs
¹/₄ teaspoon salt
1 pint whipping cream
2 tablespoons cocoa mix
¹/₂ teaspoon coffee liqueur
2 tablespoons confectioner's sugar

Add butter to hot water and boil until melted. Add granulated sugar, salt, and flour and stir vigorously until mixture leaves sides of saucepan. Remove from heat. Quickly beat in, 1 at a time, the 4 eggs. Continue beating until thick and smooth. Grease baking sheet lightly and drop heaped tablespoons of this dough, 2 inches apart, on baking sheet. Heat oven to 425° and bake puffs for 15 minutes. Reduce heat to 350° and bake a few minutes longer until golden brown. Remove to rack to cool completely. Whip cream until stiff. Mix in cocoa, 1 tablepoon confectioner's sugar, and the coffee liqueur. Cut off tops of puffs and fill with chocolate-coffee cream and replace tops. Sprinkle tops with remaining confectioner's sugar. Refrigerate until serving time.

MENU 21

FRESH MUSHROOM CANAPES ON TOAST
INDIVIDUAL SPINACH CASSEROLES
COLE SLAW SALAD
COFFEE-BRANDY CREAM IN GLASSES

This is a somewhat unusual menu and quite an adventure for conventional guests. Preparation time is appealing since it will take no longer than 45 minutes to prepare.

HELPFUL HINT

Many people wonder why fresh fruits and vegetables on the market are waxed. Waxing reduces moisture loss and gives produce a brighter appearance. It is said that the wax is nontoxic and safe to eat but I would like to tell you how you can remove this wax. Place the fruit or vegetable in the freezer for a few minutes, just long enough to chill the outside but not to freeze it. The thin layer of wax can then be easily cracked and peeled off.

FRESH MUSHROOM CANAPES ON TOAST

Wash and dry mushroom caps. Fry them in butter on both sides. Set on broiler tray. Sprinkle with onion salt, pepper, chopped parsley, and lastly with Parmesan cheese. Broil briefly until brown and serve on toast triangles (crusts removed from toast). Garnish with parsley sprigs.

1 pound large fresh mushrooms
2 ounces butter
1/2 cup chopped parsley
1/2 cup grated Parmesan cheese
4 slices toast
onion salt and pepper to taste
a few fresh parsley sprigs

INDIVIDUAL SPINACH CASSEROLES

Take 1/2 ounce of the margarine and grease four individual casseroles (small). Sprinkle each with chopped parsley. Divide well-drained chopped spinach into the four dishes. Place one raw egg over spinach in each dish.

To make the sauce, melt remaining 2 ounces of margarine, add flour, and stir until smooth. Add milk and boil, stirring all the time until sauce thickens. Add grated cheese and stir until smooth and cheese is melted. Take off stove, add mustard, onion salt, and pepper. Spoon sauce carefully over raw eggs, making sure that eggs are lightly covered. Place casseroles uncovered in moderate preheated oven (350°) and bake until they bubble and are lightly browned—approximately 15 to 20 minutes. Do not overbake since you do not want eggs to be hard.

2 1/2 ounces margarine
1/2 cup chopped parsley
4 eggs
2 pounds spinach, cooked, drained, and chopped or
1 package frozen spinach
2 tablespoons flour
1 cup grated cheddar cheese
1 1/4 cups milk
1 teaspoon mustard
onion salt and pepper to taste

COLE SLAW SALAD

Shred cabbage and grate carrot. Mix and add boiling water. Add vinegar, oil, onion salt, pepper and sugar. Add dill weed and caraway seed. Allow to marinate for 1 hour. Adjust taste, drain, and serve on individual salad plates.

1 small green cabbage
1 fresh carrot
1/2 cup boiling water
1 teaspoon caraway seed
3/4 cup salad oil
1/2 cup vinegar
1 teaspoon chopped dill weed
onion salt, pepper, and sugar to taste

COFFEE-BRANDY CREAM IN GLASSES

1 cup instant coffee, double
   strength
18 large marshmallows
1 pint whipping cream
½ teaspoon brandy
1 cup chocolate curls shaved off
   sweet chocolate bar with sharp
   knife or vegetable parer

Place coffee in double boiler and add marshmallows. Boil, stirring all the time until all are melted. Place coffee-marshmallow mixture in refrigerator and check after 20 minutes. Meanwhile whip cream and add brandy. When coffee-marshmallow mixture has barely started to thicken, add whipped cream. Fill decorative glasses and garnish with chocolate curls. Return glasses to refrigerator until mixture is firm and cold.

MENU 22

ICED FRESH FRUIT SOUP
PROTEIN-NUT LOAF
CHIVE SAUCE
FRESH GREEN BEANS
BUTTERED HERB NOODLES
APPLE CHEESE PIE

The fruit soup, which is served first, lends itself to spring or summer but tastes delicious any day of the year.

HELPFUL HINT
All ingredients for a pie crust should be cold. As much as possible, avoid using your hands when handling dough. You can work with a knife, fork, or foil paper. If you observe these simple rules the results will be most rewarding.

ICED FRESH FRUIT SOUP

Wash or defrost raspberries. Add 4 cups of water. Add stoned, peeled peaches, cherries, lemon juice, and the oranges. Boil slowly for 45 minutes. Strain, add red vegetable food color and sugar to taste. Cool slightly and add vanilla pudding by mixing pudding powder with a little soup and adding to cooled soup. Boil up mixture briefly, stirring all the time. Chill. Add grapes before serving.

2 packages frozen or 1 pound fresh
*   raspberries*
2 peaches
4 cups water
1/2 pound fresh black cherries,
*   pitted*
juice of 1 lemon
4 oranges, peeled and sectioned
1 teaspoon red vegetable food color
sugar to taste
1 cup seedless grapes
1 package vanilla pudding

PROTEIN-NUT LOAF

Fry chopped onions and cauliflower in margarine until golden brown. Mix together with rest of ingredients. Shape into loaf and place on buttered baking pan. Bake in moderate oven (350°) until firm and golden brown, approximately 30 minutes.

1 cup chopped onion
1 cup grated cauliflower
1 ounce margarine
1 cup ground cashew nuts
1 cup grated cheddar cheese
1/2 cup chopped parsley
1 teaspoon Savita
2 eggs
onion salt and pepper

CHIVE SAUCE

Melt butter. Add flour and stir until smooth. Add water and lemon juice and Washington Broth, and boil up until sauce thickens, stirring all the time. Add seasonings and chives.

2 ounces butter
2 tablespoons flour
1³/₄ cups water
juice of 1/2 lemon
1/2 cup chopped chives
1 package chicken-flavored Wash-
*   ington Broth*
onion salt, pepper, sugar to taste

FRESH GREEN BEANS

Cut off ends from string beans and cut beans into bite-sized pieces. Fry onions in butter. Add beans and enough water to cover. Boil slowly until beans are tender and most of the water is absorbed. Drain excess water and add rest of ingredients.

2 pounds fresh string beans
1/2 cup chopped onion
1 ounce butter
2 tablespoons chopped parsley
onion salt and pepper to taste

HERB NOODLES

1 pound noodles
3 cups boiling water
1 ounce butter
*1 tablespoon chopped thyme, or 1
     teaspoon dried*
*2 tablespoons grated Parmesan
     cheese*
onion salt and pepper to taste

Add noodles to boiling water and cook until tender, but be sure not to overcook. Strain noodles and place in dish. Toss with melted butter, thyme, Parmesan cheese, onion salt, and pepper.

APPLE CHEESE PIE

PASTRY
1 cup flour
3 tablespoons brown sugar
¼ pound margarine

FILLING
4 eating apples
¼ cup currants
2 tablespoons sugar

TOPPING
1 8-ounce package cream cheese
½ cup granulated sugar
1 teaspoon grated lemon peel
1 teaspoon vanilla essence
2 eggs

Combine sugar with sifted flour and cut in the margarine in very small pieces. Mix with your fingers until pastry resembles cornmeal. Press over bottom and sides of 9- or 10-inch pie plate.

Peel, core, and cut apples into slices and place in pie dish in circles, overlapping each slice slightly. Sprinkle with sugar and currants.

To make topping, beat ingredients in electric mixer until smooth and pour over apples evenly. Bake in moderate oven (350°) for approximately 30 minutes until light brown. Cool.

MENU 23

AVOCADO AND CITRUS SALAD
VEGETABLE PIE AU GRATIN
BROILED FRESH PINEAPPLE RINGS
COFFEE TRIFLE

I should mention that the dessert in this menu is my version of the traditional English trifle which is made without gelatin and uses a custard over sponge cake and fruit. Naturally, I am prejudiced in favor of my version.

HELPFUL HINT
If you would like a good recipe for a light wine punch, mix one part rosé wine with two parts fresh apple juice, and chill.

AVOCADO AND CITRUS SALAD

Peel and slice avocados and prepare grapefruit sections. Arrange on washed, shredded lettuce. Garnish with watercress. Make dressing by mixing grapefruit juice, honey, onion salt, and pepper; spoon over avocado slices so that they do not discolor.

2 avocados
3 large pink grapefruits
1 lettuce
1 small bunch watercress
1/2 cup grapefruit juice (reserved from grapefruit)
1/4 cup honey
onion salt and pepper to taste

VEGETABLE PIE AU GRATIN

Combine 1 cup sifted flour, onion salt and pepper. Cut in 1/4 pound margarine and work with fingers until mixture resembles cornmeal. Press pastry over bottom and sides of 9-inch pie dish. Set aside.

Cut vegetables into bite-sized pieces and spread over entire bottom of pastry shell.

To make the sauce, melt margarine, add flour and stir until smooth. Add milk and 1 cup grated cheese. Boil briefly, stirring all the time. Remove from stove and add mustard, onion salt, and pepper. Pour over vegetables in pastry shell, making sure that all of the vegetables are covered. Sprinkle with remaining grated cheese and bake in 350° oven until light brown—about 30 minutes —and vegetables are tender.

PASTRY
1 cup flour
1/4 pound margarine
onion salt and pepper to taste

VEGETABLES
1 small cauliflower
1 peeled tomato
2 small zucchinis
1/2 cup chopped green onions
onion salt and pepper to taste

CHEESE SAUCE
2 cups grated cheddar cheese
1 1/2 cups milk
3 ounces margarine
2 1/2 tablespoons flour
1 teaspoon mustard
onion salt and pepper to taste

BROILED FRESH PINEAPPLE RINGS

Slice pineapple into 1/4-inch slices, discarding both ends. Remove outside rind and inner core as neatly as possible. Place slices on broiling pan and baste with syrup-sugar mixture. Broil about 5 minutes. Serve with vegetable pie.

1 fresh pineapple
1/2 cup maple syrup
2 teaspoons brown sugar

COFFEE TRIFLE

1 package lady fingers
1/4 cup sweet sherry
1 pound fresh pears or other fruit
    in season
1 package raspberry gelatin
1 pint whipping cream
1/2 teaspoon vanilla extract
2 teaspoons granulated sugar
2 teaspoons powdered coffee
4 ounces chocolate curls

Place lady fingers in deep glass dish. Sprinkle sweet sherry over them. Peel and slice up fruit and place generous layer over lady fingers. Prepare gelatin according to package and pour over fruit. Allow to set in refrigerator. Whip cream, add powdered coffee, sugar, and vanilla, and spread over set gelatin. Decorate with chocolate curls shaved off sweet chocolate bar with sharp knife and chill.

MENU 24

FRESH FRUIT CUP
SPINACH-BRAZIL NUT ROULADE
CREAMED ARTICHOKE BOTTOMS
MOLDED GRAPEFRUIT SALAD
WITH CUCUMBER SAUCE
SUNKIST ICEBOX CAKE

This menu looks as pretty as it is tasty. My photographers helped to eat up the food after pictures were taken and I hope the comments of your guests are as heartwarming as theirs. I will admit this menu is rather time consuming, but let me reassure you, it is well worth the effort.

HELPFUL HINT

When a recipe calls for firmly packed brown sugar, spoon the sugar into the measure a little at a time, packing it down firmly with back of spoon. The sugar will stand up in a mold when turned out.

FRESH FRUIT CUP

Wash and grate apples up to core. Add lemon juice. Prepare oranges like grapefruit by cutting in half and taking out sections. Add to apples. Cut up banana and add. Mix gently with honey and sugar. Chill. Before serving in individual dishes, add almonds.

2 eating apples
3 oranges
juice of 1/2 lemon
1 tablespoon roasted almonds, slivered
1 tablespoon honey
1 tablespoon brown sugar
1 banana

SPINACH-BRAZIL NUT ROULADE

Wash spinach, remove stems, and boil in a little water. After 5 minutes drain well, chop, and place in mixing bowl. Add 1 ounce of butter, melted, and some onion salt. Beat in the 8 egg yolks. Then beat the whites of the eggs until stiff and add to spinach mixture. Oil a cookie sheet with 1/2 inch sides and line with waxed paper. Butter the paper well and sprinkle with bread crumbs. Spread spinach mixture over bread crumbs evenly and sprinkle Parmesan cheese over all. Bake in moderate (350°) oven for 15 minutes.

Meanwhile, prepare stuffing. Fry mushrooms and onion in 3 ounces butter for a few minutes. Sprinkle with the flour and stir. Add milk and stir until it thickens. Add sherry, nuts, parsley, onion salt, and pepper. Remove spinach from oven and cover with a large sheet of buttered waxed paper (butter on the spinach side). Invert gently on a heatable platter. Remove top waxed paper slowly. Spread stuffing evenly over spinach. Carefully pull under waxed paper, making the roulade roll up on itself. Warm up again in oven before serving.

2 pounds fresh spinach
4 ounces butter
8 eggs, separated
1 small chopped onion
3 tablespoons bread crumbs
1/2 pound sliced mushrooms
2 tablespoons flour
3/4 cup milk
1/2 cup chopped Brazil nuts
4 tablespoons grated Parmesan cheese
1 tablespoon parsley
1/4 cup sherry
oil, just enough to oil cookie sheet
onion salt and pepper to taste

CREAMED ARTICHOKE BOTTOMS

Add flour to melted butter, stir until smooth. Add 2 cups of water, Washington Broth, parsley, onion salt, and pepper. Bring to boil, stirring all the time until mixture thickens. Add artichoke bottoms and mix.

2 ounces butter
2 tablespoons flour
2 cups water
2 tablespoons chopped parsley
1 package chicken-flavored Washington Broth
onion salt and pepper to taste
3 cups artichoke bottoms

MOLDED GRAPEFRUIT SALAD WITH CUCUMBER SAUCE

1 3-ounce package lime gelatin
1 cup boiling water
½ cup grapefruit juice
½ cup mayonnaise
1 cup fresh grapefruit sections
½ cup celery, chopped
lettuce for individual salad beds

CUCUMBER SAUCE

1 cup mayonnaise
juice of ½ lemon
1 cup cucumber, diced without skin
    and seeds
1 tablespoon honey
1 teaspoon dill weed
onion salt and pepper

Dissolve gelatin in boiling water. Add grapefruit juice and mayonnaise and blend in electric mixer. Pour into bowl and chill until partially set. Beat in mixer once again. Fold in grapefruit sections and celery. Pour into muffin pan to make 6 or 8 individual molds and chill. Place shredded lettuce on individual salad plates and turn out gelatin molds, one on each plate, and serve with cucumber sauce.

To make the sauce, mix all ingredients thoroughly until perfectly smooth, adding cucumber last.

SUNKIST ICEBOX CAKE

1½ cups orange juice
1 envelope gelatin
⅓ cup granulated sugar
36 small marshmallows
1 can mandarin oranges, drained
1 pint heavy cream, whhipped
2 packages lady fingers
chocolate curls shaved off sweet
    chocolate bar with sharp knife
    or vegetable parer

Sprinkle gelatin over ¼ cup orange juice. Allow to stand for 15 minutes. Place in pan and heat slowly, stirring until gelatin is all dissolved. Add sugar and 1¼ cups orange juice; mix well over heat. Cool in refrigerator. When mixture is slightly congealed, take out and beat until fluffy. Add mandarin orange sections, miniature marshmallows, and finally whipped cream. Line bottom and sides of spring-form cake pan with lady fingers. Fill halfway with orange mixture. Put layer of remaining lady fingers and fill up with remaining orange mixture. Chill until firm and decorate with chocolate curls.

MENU 25

TOMATO SOUP
RAW SALAD PLATE
BAKED POTATOES AU GRATIN
PEAR CRUMB PIE

The raw salad plate served as a main course is usually the hardest thing to get used to when breaking away from the conventional diet. There are, of course, a great many exciting varieties of salads, but for the moment I will let you concentrate on this one and I wish you success if this is your first attempt.

HELPFUL HINT
To avoid eggs cracking when boiled, warm the egg shells under lukewarm water before placing them in boiling water.

TOMATO SOUP

Cut up onions, celery, and tomatoes, and fry in margarine for 5 minutes. Add peeled, chopped potatoes, 4 cups water, Savita, Washington Broth, and oregano. Boil slowly for 1 hour. Strain and add onion salt, pepper, and sugar to taste. Sprinkle with chopped chives and serve.

12 tomatoes, peeled
2 onions
2 celery sticks
2 ounces margarine
2 potatoes
4 cups water
4 packages chicken-flavored Washington Broth
1/2 teaspoon Savita
1/4 teaspoon oregano
onion salt, pepper, sugar to taste
2 tablespoons chopped chives

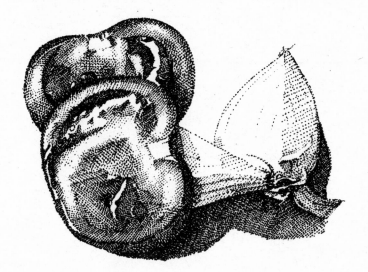

RAW SALAD PLATE

Divide washed, dried lettuce over four individual salad plates. On each plate, place a heap of ground nuts mixed with chopped dates in center. Around this place sliced cucumber, sliced tomatoes, grated cauliflower, 1/2 an egg, grated beets, grated carrot. Sprinkle dill weed over tomatoes.

1 head lettuce
1 cup dates, pitted and chopped
1 cup finely ground Brazil nuts
4 tomatoes
1/2 medium-sized cauliflower, grated
1 small thinly sliced cucumber
2 raw beets
2 carrots
2 teaspoons dill weed
2 hard-boiled eggs, quartered or sliced
onion salt to taste

DRESSING

1 cup mayonnaise
juice of 1 lemon
1 teaspoon parsley, chopped
1 tablespoon honey
onion salt and pepper to taste

Mix all ingredients together.

BAKED POTATOES AU GRATIN

4 large potatoes
1 cup grated cheddar cheese
1 ounce butter
onion salt and pepper to taste
1/2 cup sesame seeds

Bake potatoes in oven (425°) for 1 hour. When slightly cooled, cut in halves and scoop out insides, reserving empty shells. Mash potato with butter, grated cheese, onion salt, and pepper until very smooth. Refill potato halves, smooth tops of potatoes with fork and sprinkle with sesame seed. Before serving, broil until brown and serve hot with salad plate.

PEAR-CRUMB PIE

2 cups plus 2 tablespoons flour
1/2 pound margarine
1 cup granulated sugar
4 cups pears, firm-ripe, sliced
3/4 cup chopped pecans
1/2 teaspoon cinnamon
juice of 1 lemon

Prepare crust by combining 1/4 cup sugar with 1 cup of sifted flour, and cut in 1/4 pound of margarine. Work margarine into flour with fingers until mixture resembles cornmeal. Press pastry over bottom and sides of greased pie plate and set aside.

For the filling, mix sliced pears with 1/4 cup of sugar, lemon juice and 2 tablespoons of flour. Place in pie shell.

For topping, blend rest of flour, pecans, sugar, and cinnamon. Melt remaining margarine, toss hot over flour mixture and mix with fork while pouring, forming crumbs. Spread over pears until all are covered. Bake for about 30 minutes in 375° oven until pastry is cooked and crumbs lightly browned.

MENU 26

AVOCADO SOUP WITH SESAME STICKS
CHEESE AND ONION PASTRY SQUARES
WITH CHIVE SAUCE
ZUCCHINI AND TOMATO VEGETABLE
APPLE-ORANGE BETTY

Here we have a luscious but not a difficult dinner. Culinary art is one of the oldest arts. What has changed its application over the years is the knowledge and research of food values. Of course living conditions have changed also, especially the tools with which we work. The good dietician has to apply this knowledge, which is constantly growing.

HELPFUL HINT
Celery curls look decorative on salads, platters, or vegetable dips. Here is a fun way to make them.

Cut stalks of celery into short lengths—say 4 inches. Slit each end of cut pieces into even, narrow strips, leaving about ½ inch solid in center. Place in ice water to allow ends to curl.

AVOCADO SOUP WITH SESAME STICKS

Puree peeled and stoned avocados with fork and then in electric mixer. Add ½ cup water, garlic salt, lime juice. When thoroughly creamy, add another cup water, light cream, onion salt, pepper, and sugar, and blend again. Serve cold over chopped chives.

Make sesame sticks by cutting crust off bread slices and flattening bread with rolling pin. Butter on both sides. Cut each slice in half. Roll up long side of each ½ slice of bread, which will stick to itself. Mix sesame seeds with a little onion salt and dip rolls into this mixture. Bake on cookie sheet in moderate oven (350°) for about 15 minutes until golden. May be served warm with cold soup.

3 ripe, soft avocados
1½ cups water
2 teaspoons lime juice
1 cup light cream
½ cup chopped chives
½ teaspoon garlic salt
8 slices bread
½ cup sesame seeds
1 ounce butter
onion salt, pepper, pinch of sugar

CHEESE AND ONION PASTRY SQUARES

Grate butter into sifted flour, reserving just enough butter to grease cookie sheet. Mix flour and butter with your fingers until mixture resembles cornmeal. Add grated cheese, distributing evenly into dough with fork. Add eggs, sage, onion salt, pepper, and mix up well. Grease cookie sheet. Flour your hands and press cheese dough onto cookie sheet, spreading it out evenly. Sprinkle with chopped green onions and bake in moderate oven (350°) for about 30 minutes or until light brown. Cut into squares and serve hot with chive sauce.

4 ounces butter
1½ cups flour
3 eggs
1 cup grated cheddar cheese
1 cup chopped green onions
¼ teaspoon sage
onion salt and pepper to taste

CHIVE SAUCE

Add flour to melted margarine and stir, over heat, until smooth. Add milk, stirring all the time until sauce thickens. Add chives and seasoning.

2 ounces margarine
2 tablespoons flour
1½ cups milk
½ cup chopped chives
onion salt and pepper to taste

ZUCCHINI AND TOMATOES

6 small zucchinis
2 firm tomatoes
½ cup chopped parsley
1 ounce butter
1 teaspoon ketchup
onion salt and pepper to taste

Wash and slice zucchinis and tomatoes. Melt butter and add vegetables, parsley, seasoning, and ketchup. Cover and simmer for 5 minutes.

APPLE-ORANGE BETTY

5 eating apples
juice of 1 lemon
juice of 2 oranges
2 tablespoons honey
3 ounces butter
4 tablespoons flour
4 tablespoons brown sugar
½ cup chopped pecans

Peel, core, and slice apples. Add honey, lemon, and orange juice. Simmer for 15 minutes. Put in ovenproof dish with juice if any is left after cooking. Mix flour, sugar, and nuts with fork. Melt butter and pour very hot over flour, mixing with fork as you pour, forming crumbs. Sprinkle over apple mixture and bake in moderate oven (350°) about 30 minutes until light brown on top.

MENU 27

MINTED MELON BALLS
MUSHROOM QUICHE
BRUSSEL SPROUTS WITH CHESTNUTS
PORT WINE MOLD SALAD
APRICOT SPONGE

Cooking represents a large part of most women's lives. To some it is a chore and to others it brings pleasure. To me it is a way to make people happy, and what is more fulfilling than that? The following dinner is fun to prepare and will please most palates.

HELPFUL HINT
Add a little milk to the water in which cauliflower is cooking, so it remains white. White looks so much more attractive than the dirty grey it may otherwise become.

MINTED MELON BALLS

Mix melon balls with lemon juice and sugar. Serve in glasses and decorate with mint.

melon of your choice
juice of 1/2 lemon
1 tablespoon brown sugar
4 sprigs fresh mint

MUSHROOM QUICHE

Make pastry by grating 4 ounces margarine into sifted flour. Add salt and pepper and work with your fingers until mixture resembles cornmeal. Add Savita water and mix with knife until it forms into a doughlike mixture. When very well blended, press into a 9-inch pie plate. Prick pastry with fork to avoid bubbles, and bake in 350° oven about 15 minutes until barely cooked. Set aside. Melt remaining margarine in skillet. Add onions, mushrooms, lemon juice, onion salt, and pepper, and cook for a few minutes stirring until liquid is absorbed. Beat eggs and cream together. Mix with onion-mushroom mixture and pour into cooked pie shell. Sprinkle top with grated cheese and bake for 30 minutes in 350° oven until quiche is puffy and brown on top and knife comes out clean.

1 1/2 cups flour
6 ounces margarine
1/2 teaspoon Savita, dissolved in 3
*   tablespoons water*
1/2 cup chopped onion
2 cups mushrooms, chopped
1 teaspoon lemon juice
4 eggs
1 cup light cream
3/4 cup grated Swiss cheese
onion salt and pepper to taste

BRUSSEL SPROUTS AND CHESTNUTS

Drain chestnuts. Add flour to melted butter and stir, over heat, until smooth. Add water and bring to boil, stirring all the time until sauce thickens. Add sprouts and seasoning and simmer for 15 minutes in covered pan, stirring occasionally. Add chestnuts.

3 cups brussel sprouts
1 small can chestnuts
1 ounce butter
1 tablespoon flour
1/2 cup water
onion salt and pepper to taste

PORT WINE MOLD SALAD

1¼ cups sparkling water
1 envelope gelatin
½ cup ruby port wine
½ cup sugar
1 cup slivered almonds
½ cup mayonnaise
1 tablespoon lemon juice
1 tablespoon oil
1 head lettuce

Lightly oil four individual molds. Prepare gelatin by pouring ½ cup sparkling water into small bowl. Sprinkle gelatin over it. Allow to stand 5 minutes to soften gelatin. Meanwhile, mix remaining sparkling water, wine, ¼ cup sugar. Place gelatin mixture in double boiler and heat until gelatin is dissolved, stirring all the time. Blend thoroughly with wine mixture and heat some more, stirring until all is well mixed. Put slivered almonds in molds. Pour gelatin mixture over almonds and chill in refrigerator. Mix mayonnaise with lemon juice and remaining sugar, and serve over molds which, when set, are placed on shredded lettuce.

APRICOT SPONGE

2 cups dried apricots
3 eggs
1 cup brown sugar
1 cup flour
1 teaspoon baking powder
½ cup chopped pecans
½ ounce butter
2 tablespoons confectioner's sugar
¼ teaspoon allspice

Soak apricots in warm water for 1 hour and then boil until tender. Drain and strain, making puree. Beat eggs and sugar, add flour, baking powder, apricot puree, nuts, and mix well. Bake in greased flat pan in moderate oven (350°) for about 30 minutes or until light brown. Cool and cut into small squares and sprinkle with confectioner's sugar.

MENU 28

TOMATO AND EGG YOLK SALAD
STUFFED GREEN PEPPERS
SWEET CORN OFF THE COB
BROILED MUSHROOMS
NUT MERINGUE TORTE

No more rhapsodizing about the delectability of my menus; by now you will have made up your own mind. If you feel like cooking "a la carte" for a change and switch around menus and recipes, who is to stop you? Vegetarian cooking lends itself to using your imagination, once you understand the basic principles of this kind of diet, and if you feel so inclined, do some experimenting of your own. After all, that is how I developed all of my recipes.

HELPFUL HINT
If you are cooking vegetables with a strong odor, you can absorb the odor while cooking by keeping a small can (a frozen orange juice can will do nicely) half-filled with vinegar near the stove.

TOMATO AND EGG YOLK SALAD

Wash and dry lettuce and arrange leaves on 4 plates. Pour boiling water over tomatoes. Remove water after 1 minute and peel off skin. Cut thin slices and arrange over lettuce. Put hard-boiled yolks of eggs through ricer and sprinkle over tomatoes. Make a little French dressing by mixing oil, vinegar, dill, onion salt, pepper and a little sugar and pour over salads.

lettuce leaves for salad beds
4 large, firm tomatoes
4 hard-boiled eggs
1 teaspoon dill weed
1/2 cup oil
1/4 cup vinegar
onion salt, pepper, sugar to taste

STUFFED GREEN PEPPERS

Slice stem ends from peppers and remove seeds. Drop peppers into boiling water and cook for 3 minutes. Drain off water and set aside. Openings are at stem end; cut thin slice off opposite end to have them stand flat. Make sauce by melting 2 ounces butter, adding flour and stirring until smooth. Add milk, stirring all the time until sauce thickens. Set aside. Fry onion in remaining butter until golden. To this, add cheddar cheese, cooked rice, parsley, curry powder, garlic salt, ground cashews, raisins, onion salt, and pepper. Add this mixture to white sauce. Spoon into peppers and top with Parmesan cheese. Stand stuffed peppers in a shallow baking dish. Add 1/2 inch water to dish and bake uncovered in a 350° oven for 30 minutes or until brown on top.

4 green peppers
2 1/2 ounces butter
2 tablespoons flour
1 cup milk
1 chopped onion
1/2 cup grated cheddar cheese
1 1/2 cups cooked brown rice
1 tablespoon chopped parsley
1 teaspoon curry powder
1/4 teaspoon garlic salt
1 cup finely ground cashew nuts
onion salt and pepper to taste
1/3 cup golden seedless raisins
1/2 cup grated parmesan cheese

SWEET CORN OFF THE COB

Husk corn and cook in boiling water for 15 minutes. Drain and cool. With sharp knife, slice corn kernels off the cob into saucepan. Add melted butter, onion salt, and pepper.

6 fresh ears of corn
1 ounce butter
onion salt and pepper to taste

BROILED MUSHROOMS

16 large fresh mushrooms
1½ ounces butter
2 tablespoons chopped parsley
1 tablespoon Worcestershire sauce
onion salt and pepper to taste

Remove stems, and wash and dry mushrooms. Place on greased broiling pan. Mix melted butter, Worcestershire sauce, parsley, onion salt, and pepper and baste mushroom caps. Broil for a few minutes. Turn and baste other side and broil for another minute.

NUT MERINGUE TORTE

3 egg whites
½ teaspoon vanilla
½ cup + 1 teaspoon sugar
1 cup finely ground almonds
½ pint whipping cream
1 teaspoon powdered coffee
½ teaspoon kirsch
1 can mandarin oranges
¼ teaspoon ginger
1 teaspoon cornstarch

Beat egg whites until stiff. Add vanilla, ½ cup sugar, ground almonds. Mix well and bake in greased 9-inch pie plate at 325° for 30 minutes, or until just light brown. When cool, cover with whipped cream to which you have added the powdered coffee, kirsch, and teaspoon of sugar. Put mandarin oranges in saucepan. Mix cornstarch with a little of the mandarin juice and add to mandarins. Add ginger, boil up very briefly, stirring gently. Cool for ½ hour at least and spoon cool mandarin glaze over coffee cream, covering the whole top.

MENU 29

AVOCADO-MELON SALAD
WITH STRAWBERRY DRESSING
PROTEIN KEBABS
BARLEY PILAF
BAKED CARROTS
PINEAPPLE CREAM CHEESE BROIL

When you serve these attractive protein kebabs, place the skewers right on dinner plate and guests or family will remove their contents with their forks. Serving the complete skewer on the dinner plate looks more appealing.

HELPFUL HINT

In case fingers get a little sticky, use pretty finger bowls and mini-towels. The towels can be passed after the main course, but the finger bowls enhance the table setting, especially if you float a fresh flower in the half-filled bowls and add a very little scent to the slightly warm water.

AVOCADO-MELON SALAD WITH STRAWBERRY DRESSING

Prepare avocado and melon balls and mix with lemon juice. Make sauce by slicing washed strawberries and mixing with sour cream and sugar. If you like a more runny sauce, use a little milk to thin sour cream before adding strawberries. Shred lettuce, place avocado and melon balls on lettuce, and serve with sauce.

3 cups avocado balls
2 cups melon balls (any melon)
juice of ½ lemon
1 cup fresh strawberries, or 1 cup
*   frozen, thawed, and drained*
1 cup sour cream
2 tablespoons sugar
lettuce for salad beds

PROTEIN KEBABS

Thread vegetables on metal skewers, reserving cheese cubes. Mix oil, vinegar, and seasonings. Baste skewers and broil on foil-covered broiling pan, turning and basting until all sides are cooked. When cooked, add cheese cubes and broil again very briefly, just long enough to heat cheese without melting it too much. Serve with barley pilaf and baked carrots.

16 mushroom caps
12 zucchinis cut in ½-inch slices
4 cherry tomatoes
4 pearl onions
8 cubes Swiss cheese
¼ cup oil
2 tablespoons vinegar
onion salt, garlic salt, pepper to
*   taste*

BARLEY PILAF

2 ounces butter
1 chopped onion
½ cup chopped chives
1 cup barley
2 cups water
1 package chicken-flavored Wash-
    ington Broth
1 teaspoon Savita
onion salt and pepper to taste

Fry chopped onion and chives in melted butter. Add barley, 2 cups water, Washington Savita, and seasonings. Boil slowly until barley is tender, about 30 minutes. Most of the water will be absorbed.

BAKED CARROTS

8 long carrots
½ cup water
2 ounces butter
2 tablespoons brown sugar
¼ teaspoon ground ginger

Scrape and wash whole carrots. Cut into lengthwise halves. Place in buttered ovenproof dish. Add ½ cup water. Sprinkle with sugar and ginger, and dot with butter. Bake in uncovered dish at 350° for about 45 minutes or until tender and lightly browned.

PINEAPPLE
CREAM CHEESE BROIL

1 pineapple
1 8-ounce package cream cheese,
    softened at room temperature
1 teaspoon brown sugar
½ teaspoon vanilla
1 teaspoon cinnamon

Cut pineapple into slices, trim rind, and remove core. Mix softened cream cheese with sugar and vanilla. Spread over pineapple slices. Sprinkle with cinnamon and broil. Serve warm and slightly browned.

MENU 30

MIXED CUCUMBER, TOMATO, AND
WATERCRESS SALAD
BRAZIL NUT FRITTERS
STUFFED ONIONS
THYME SAUCE
CREAMED CARROTS
FLAMING APPLES WITH ALMONDS

A flaming dessert is always fun to serve and this is a very simple one.

HELPFUL HINTS
The efficient cook takes inventory of her kitchen once a week. All kitchen chores are so much faster and simpler if basics are on hand and equipment checked. Always be sure to have your herb jars filled unless of course you have fresh herbs in your garden and can pick them whenever the need occurs.

Do you have a talent for producing rhymes? To warm up conversation for your dinner party, write a two- or three-line rhyme as a place card for each person at the dinner table. Here is an example:

"Hilda and Eric dwell in your town.
You are an artist of renown."

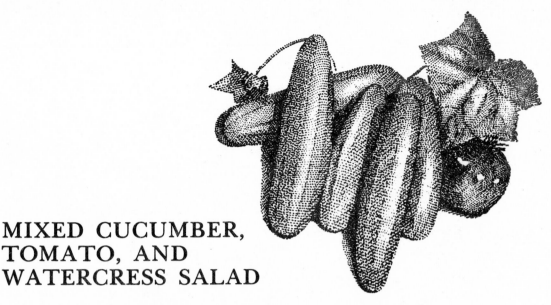

MIXED CUCUMBER, TOMATO, AND WATERCRESS SALAD

Slice cucumber very thin, add peeled, sliced tomatoes. Peel tomatoes by pouring boiling water over them; take out after ½ minute. Make French dressing by mixing oil, vinegar, dill weed, seasonings. Pour over individual salads. Decorate with washed watercress.

1 cucumber
3 tomatoes
1 small bunch watercress
¼ cup oil
1 tablespoon vinegar
1 teaspoon dill weed
onion salt, pepper, sugar to taste

BRAZIL NUT FRITTERS

Make fritter batter by mixing eggs, flour, and soya flour, milk, 1 ounce melted butter, parsley, onion salt, and pepper. Add chopped nuts. Fry chopped onions in remaining butter and add to batter. Heat oil and drop 2 tablespoons of batter at a time into pan and cook until brown on both sides. Serve with thyme sauce and stuffed onions.

1 cup Brazil nuts, chopped into
*   small pieces*
1 chopped onion
2 ounces butter
1 cup flour
1 teaspoon soya flour
2 teaspoons chopped parsley
⅔ cup milk
2 eggs
½ cup oil
onion salt and pepper to taste

THYME SAUCE

Add flour to melted margarine and stir until smooth. Add milk and bring to boil, stirring all the time until it thickens. Add seasoning and serve over fritters.

2 ounces margarine
2 tablespoons flour
1¼ cups milk
1 package chicken-flavored Wash-
*   ington Broth*
1 teaspoon thyme
onion salt and pepper to taste

STUFFED ONIONS

4 peeled onions
2 ounces margarine
2 tablespoons grated Parmesan
    cheese
1/2 cup bread crumbs
aluminum foil for baking onions

Scoop out center of each onion with sharp knife, leaving a fairly thin shell. Chop up scooped-out onion and fry until golden in margarine. Add remaining ingredients and mix well; fill onion shells. Cut a square of aluminum foil for each onion, large enough so that an airtight package can be made of each. Bake foil-onion packages in an ovenproof dish for 1 hour at 375°. Serve with fritters.

CREAMED CARROTS

3 cups thin sliced carrots
1 ounce butter
1/2 cup water
1/2 teaspoon ground ginger
1/2 teaspoon brown sugar

Cook carrots in melted butter for 2 minutes. Add 1/2 cup water, ginger, sugar. Boil slowly for 15 minutes in covered pan.

FLAMING APPLES WITH ALMONDS

1 cup blanched almonds
4 large green apples
1/2 cup seedless raisins
1/2 ounce butter
2 tablespoons brown sugar
1/4 cup rum
1/4 cup brandy

Butter shallow baking dish. Wash apples, cut into halves through middle, and core. Cut small slits in a spoke design in cut surfaces of apples. Cut a thin wedge away from each slit and place an almond in each groove lengthwise. Arrange apples cut side up in baking pan. (You may have to cut a thin slice from bottom to make apples stand flat.) Mix seedless raisins with melted butter and fill center cavities of apples. Pour 1 cup of water around apples. Sprinkle the sugar over the apples. Bake in 350° oven for approximately 30 minutes, uncovered, until apples are tender but not fallen apart. Before serving (warm), heat rum and brandy in saucepan. Place in dish on table and ignite. Spoon flaming mixture over apples at the table.

MENU 31

EGG MOLD WITH GREEN ONION SAUCE
SPAGHETTI AND NUT DUMPLINGS
IN TOMATO SAUCE
TOSSED SALAD
COFFEE ICEBOX CAKE

When your children bring their friends for dinner, what sounds more popular than a spaghetti main course?

HELPFUL HINTS

Have you remembered to provide some dinner background music? Get to know the preference of your guests, whether classical music or jazz. Play it quietly so it provides background entertainment and guests do not have to shout when engaging in conversation. Do not limit dinner music to parties; the family enjoys it also.

Do not prolong your cocktail hour beyond a reasonable dinner hour. No matter how hungry your guests are on arrival, by 9:30 P.M. they are beyond hunger pangs and your efforts to provide a tasty meal are wasted.

EGG MOLD WITH GREEN ONION SAUCE

Halve hard-boiled eggs and remove yolks into small bowl. Add mustard, chives, mayonnaise, onion salt, and pepper, and mash with fork until very fine. Refill egg whites, smoothing tops with fork, and sprinkle with a little paprika.

Prepare apple gelatin according to package and pour a little into a square pie plate—just a very thin layer. Chill. When slightly set, place stuffed eggs neatly over gelatin bed and spoon remaining gelatin over eggs. Chill in refrigerator. Before serving, cut squares around the stuffed eggs and place on individual plates and serve with green onion sauce.

Make green onion sauce by mixing sour cream with vinegar, chopped green onions, onion salt, and a little sugar to taste.

4 hard-boiled eggs
1 teaspoon mustard
1 teaspoon chopped chives
1 teaspoon mayonnaise
2 packages apple gelatin
3/4 cup chopped green onions
1 cup sour cream
1 tablespoon vinegar
onion salt, pepper, sugar, a little paprika

SPAGHETTI AND NUT DUMPLINGS IN TOMATO SAUCE

1 package spaghetti
1 cup finely ground cashew nuts
½ cup chopped fried onions
2 tablespoons chopped parsley
½ cup raw cauliflower, finely
· grated
2 eggs
½ cup bread crumbs
onion salt and pepper to taste

TOMATO SAUCE

1 can tomato puree
½ pound fresh tomatoes, chopped
1 chopped onion
1 leek, chopped or cut into thin
slices
2 packages chicken-flavored
Washington Broth
1 tablespoon spaghetti seasoning
1 ounce margarine
1 tablespoon flour
½ cup water
½ teaspoon basil
3 tablespoons grated Parmesan
cheese
½ teaspoon marjoram
onion salt, pepper, and sugar to
taste

To make dumplings, mix ground nuts, fried onions, parsley, grated cauliflower, eggs, onion salt, and pepper, and bread crumbs. Shape into small balls. Bring 3 cups of water to boil and drop nut dumplings into boiling water. Cover and cook slowly for 5 minutes until they float on top. Drain and reserve for placing on top of spaghetti dish. Cook spaghetti in boiling water to which has been added a little onion salt and pepper. When tender, drain and place in casserole.

Fry chopped onion and leek in margarine until golden. Add flour and stir until smooth. Then add tomatoes and tomato puree, and cook for 2 minutes, stirring well. Add ½ cup water, bring to boil slowly, and cook for 15 minutes, stirring all the time. Strain and add a little onion salt, pepper, and sugar to taste. Add herbs, broth and Parmesan cheese. Mix with spaghetti. Decorate top with dumplings and serve hot with tossed salad.

TOSSED SALAD

1 head lettuce
1 cup alfalfa seed sprouts
1 tomato
1/2 cup oil
1/4 cup vinegar
1 teaspoon dill
garlic salt and pepper to taste

Wash, dry, and shred lettuce. Decorate with sliced tomato and alfalfa seed sprouts, and make French dressing by mixing rest of ingredients; pour over salad. Toss at table.

COFFEE ICEBOX CAKE

1 pound marshmallows
1 cup double-strength coffee
1 pint cream, whipped
2 dozen lady fingers
1 cup chocolate curls shaved off
    sweet chocolate bar with sharp
    knife or vegetable parer

Place double-strength coffee in double boiler and add marshmallows. Bring to boil, stirring all the time until marshmallows are melted completely. Cool in refrigerator until mixture begins to set (approximately 30 minutes). Fold in whipped cream. Line bottom and sides of spring-form cake pan with lady fingers. Fill halfway with coffee cream and cover with layer of lady fingers. Add remaining coffee cream. Decorate top with chocolate curls and allow to set in refrigerator for at least 2 hours or more.

INDEX